# SELF-LOVE WORKBOOK FOR BLACK WOMEN

# SELF-LOVE WORKBOOK

## FOR

# BLACK WOMEN

### Empowering Exercises to Build Self-Compassion and Nurture Your True Self

**RACHEL JOHNSON, LMSW, MFT**

CALLISTO PUBLISHING

Copyright © 2022 by Callisto Publishing LLC
Cover and internal design © 2022 by Callisto Publishing LLC
Illustrations © ana & yvy / Creative Market
Author photo courtesy of Mylz Blake, Black Cub Production
Art Director: Lindsey Dekker
Art Producer: Janice Ackerman
Editor: Chloe Moffett
Production Editor: Rachel Taenzler
Production Manager: Jose Olivera

Published by Callisto Publishing LLC C/O Sourcebooks LLC
P.O. Box 4410, Naperville, Illinois 60567-4410
(630) 961-3900
callistopublishing.com

Printed in the United States of America.
SB 13

THIS IS DEDICATED TO ALL
THE HEALING "HOTTIES,"
"AROUND-THE-WAY GIRLS," AND
"REGULAR SMEGULAR" SISTERS.
YOU ARE SEEN, YOU ARE NOT ALONE,
YOU ARE THE INSPIRATION.

# CONTENTS

# INTRODUCTION

Hey, sis! Welcome to a small piece of your healing journey. There is something for everyone in these upcoming pages—no matter where you are. Take what you need right now and leave the rest for a different time and place. Since we will be walking through this stage of your self-love journey together, it's only right that I share a piece of who I am and what my journey has looked like thus far!

My name is Rachel Johnson, and while I am trained to do many things, my identity begins with being a cis, queer, young Black woman in this world. The largest piece of my academic background lies in the mental health field, with two master's degrees: one in social work and another in marriage and family therapy. I am the proud owner of a holistic wellness business, Half Hood Half Holistic, that centers around accessible healing for the Black community. Much of my life has been dedicated to creating and facilitating spaces for the Black community, with an emphasis on Black women. I firmly believe that healing Black women will heal the world. Black women have been and remain the caretakers of our children and our communities, so taking care of Black women helps take care of everyone.

Self-love is one of the keys to healing. Sounds easy, right? Just wake up one day and start loving yourself? For some, it may be that simple, but for many Black women, including myself, there are many levels to this "self-love" stuff. We live in a world that is still struggling to value and respect Black women, so the journey to self-love for Black women takes a bit of intentionality. I am not the spokesperson for all Black women and certainly understand what privileges I hold and how that has influenced my experience in this world, but I have held space for many Black women using the same exact exercises and activities in this book. These same exercises have helped me in my darkest times. My road to self-love has had many detours and pit stops in places like self-esteem, accountability, understanding my history, and finding my own self-worth in a world that did not readily recognize it.

Although I have used these same exercises in my workshops, in groups, and with individual clients, I want to offer that there is only so much healing work that can be done in solitude. Different levels of healing require different things. Please consider this workbook a good start or complement to other systems of support. If you are one of the many individuals struggling with depression, anxiety, and/or PTSD, there is support for you. There is no workbook designed to replace the space of a qualified medical professional or therapist. A piece of this journey will require us to walk into spaces that are uncomfortable or unfamiliar—growth can be found there. Don't know where to start? Please visit the Resources section (see page 154) for more guidance! Let's walk through this together.

# HOW TO USE THIS BOOK

am committed to showing up in every space, fully aligned and authentic with who I am—this workbook is no different. I love Black women deeply—a space I can only sit in by truly loving myself . . . all of me. I wish that deep and unconditional love for all Black women. Because we deserve it.

This workbook has been designed with two parts. Part 1 provides a glimpse of context and history for what it means to be a Black woman in the United States today, a framework of what self-love is, and the ways one can be empowered in their healing journey. Consider part 1 "laying the foundation." Part 2 is full of exercises and activities divided into pertinent themes. Consider part 2 "self-love in practice."

This book is designed to speak to different pieces of your journey at different times. I advise you to go through the workbook front to back for the first time and then revisit any pieces as you continue your journey. Please feel free to flip to specific exercises depending on what speaks to you. I recommend finding a dedicated time to focus on the content and activities. You may also want to consider finding a close friend, family member, or circle to process what may come up for you as you work through the book.

The key to this self-love journey is grace. Practice patience and grace with yourself as you work through these pages. Pause when your body feels overwhelmed. Go with your own flow; there is no race in this healing journey.

# PART I

# EMBRACING SELF-LOVE AS A BLACK WOMAN

Okay, girl, before we jump into any exercises and activities, it's important to lay a foundation. Nothing in this world exists without context and history. There are many shared experiences and underlying themes that play into the struggle of self-love for Black women. During the first several chapters of this book, my goal is to define and create a basis for what these shared experiences are. These include but are not limited to: body image, self-esteem, lack of positive representation, the sexualization of Black bodies, colorism, texturism, and sexism—to name just a few.

Acknowledging and understanding the experience we share as Black women helps bridge gaps, build safe spaces, and reduce feelings that we are alone. During the first several chapters of this book, we will explore these shared experiences and begin to shape how Black women can move closer to self-love. There are many additional resources that can be found to expand on these topics, but for now we will explore them on the surface.

# CHAPTER 1

# REFLECTING ON YOUR IDENTITY

You may wonder: "Why a self-love book for just Black women?" Self-love is a universal concept, right? It is important for everyone to embrace a self-love journey. In fact, the world would be a much better place if everyone truly loved themselves. However, the journey for Black women to embrace self-love is different. The road-blocks set up for us to navigate are unique. This chapter will explore Black womanhood from a holistic standpoint. One that highlights all of our assets as well as the ways history, society, and cultural norms inform the way Black women are viewed and view themselves. Many of our self-love road-blocks can be traced back to our lived experiences. Many of these experiences directly shape our identity and feelings of self-worth and self-love. Together we will explore concepts such as microaggressions, intergenerational traumas, inter-sectional identities, what it means to be a "strong Black woman," and more. Let's get started—I am ready when you are!

# Living as a Black Woman Today

There are many joys that come with living as a Black woman today. Many spaces we take up. Many shapes our hair and bodies conform to. The soul in our hips when we dance and the spirit in the ingredients we use when we cook. Our powers are limitless. And yet, the reality is that there are many things in life designed to limit us. The pressure to be a caretaker has taken away our ability to care for ourselves. Being seen as "superwoman" has taken away our ability to be seen as human. The pressure from society to look, walk, and talk a certain way has removed our ability to be our authentic selves and has prompted us to doubt who we are because we allow the world to change how we view ourselves.

There are many reasons why these obstacles exist today. Key ones to note are systemic prejudice and discrimination. Systemic discrimination can be defined by policies or practices—either formal or informal—that create disadvantages based on race or color. An example of this is performing background or credit checks in a hope to limit who may be eligible for a position. Because we are more likely to experience injustice and adversity in our lives, we are also more likely to see ourselves differently from our authentic selves in light of these obstacles. We doubt ourselves because we allow the world to change the view of us, for us. When the world has continued to perpetuate a standard that we are "less than," it's hard not to feel like that's true.

And so, we have been taught to live "less than" our true selves, which has negative implications for our self-esteem, self-identity, and even our physical health. According to the National Center for Biotechnology Information (NCBI), Black women are more likely to have major depressive episodes (compared to men) but half as likely to seek or be offered treatment (compared to white women). In comparison, Black women are largely at risk for heart disease and high blood pressure (49 percent over the age of forty) but are among the lowest group to even know they are at risk. What does this data mean? It means that shifting how we view ourselves could be lifesaving.

# What Being a "Strong Black Woman" Really Means

The stereotype of the "strong Black woman" can be generally defined as the assumption that Black women are emotionally, physically, and spiritually resilient with no need for assistance. It also creates an expectation that Black women are meant to give selflessly and can succeed with little or no resources. While there's no specific person to credit for the phrase, the original intent came from Black women activists in the 1800s to show another face of Black women. The version of the "strong Black woman" we see today has different context and is used as a tool to further dehumanize our experiences. And although this martyr image was born as a means to reclaim the narrative of Black women—who were historically reduced to being seen as "mammies" or sexual objects—the phrase has consequences in the present day.

For example, Black women face many traumatic experiences in the medical field because of the false narrative that we have a higher pain threshold. In today's environment, this can be seen as not offering pain medications or interventions to Black women in hospitals because of the belief that we can withstand more pain. It is also seen in the disparities of health-related deaths among Black women because our concerns are not acknowledged or believed by medical staff.

Yes, Black women are strong, but much of that strength comes from having to navigate obstacles we shouldn't have to. There is another side to Black women that is often overlooked because they are so often seen as these fearless fighters. Black women are also soft, graceful, creative, and vulnerable. Feeling like we have to consistently be strong and selfless takes away our ability to be humans with complex emotions and a need for a supportive community. Remember, there is strength in community. I recognize that it can be difficult to ask for help if you have lived life as "the strong one," but you are not alone in your experiences.

Reducing Black women to just our "strength" traps us in a box. We destroy our mental, physical, and emotional health trying to conform to this box and live up to this narrative. Instead, I invite you to consider the ways you show up strong and graceful. What are the other areas of your personality that shine bright? Are you creative, funny, compassionate? How can you begin to define yourself without "strong" being at the center? Redefine your strength in this world.

# The Intersection between Racism and Sexism

Black women exist as many things, and there are many facets of our identity that influence our experiences. There are many "isms" in this world. As Black women, we face both racism and sexism. Facing discrimination based on both gender and race is tough. Other identities making up your social location—how you exist in this world—such as disability, neurodivergence, social class, sexual orientation, and religious affiliation can add additional layers of complexity to your experience as well. An intersectional framework takes all these aspects of identity into account. Having to navigate spaces that are inherently white, able-bodied, and male dominated is exhausting and requires a form of labor that is not often recognized.

As a Black woman, having to balance both your identity as a woman and your identity as a Black person is complex. Being in at least two subgroups that have been deemed "less than" further complicates how we see ourselves in this world. There may be moments where you feel as if you have to choose one identity over another or completely sacrifice pieces of that community as a means of survival.

Navigating these spaces and figuring out how you wish to identify without the filters or influences of the world is a challenge and can pose a threat to how you view and love yourself. It's often difficult to be in community with women who don't understand the "Black experience" and, by the same token, still have to navigate the patriarchal ideas that influence our relationships with Black men. It can be true for many that at different times, different pieces of our identities do not serve us fully when separated. For example, there are movements that center women, such as the "Me Too" movement (although this was created by a Black woman) or advocacy for reproductive rights, that fail to include the voices and experiences of Black women.

# RACIAL INJUSTICE AND
# SYSTEMIC INEQUALITY

W hen we talk about systemic inequality, we're talking about the policies and practices that exist in systems that are born from or influenced by bias. They're not caused by individual actions but continuous actions happening daily within these systems. Many spaces have been historically set up to keep Black women among the bottom ranks, including in the workplace, at home, in church, and even in peer groups. Both real and perceived power dynamics position Black women to be systematically disadvantaged. We can see these inequalities and disadvantages in pay gaps, gender roles, advocating for proper health care for ourselves, navigating academic or professional spaces, or even the way we raise our children from a survival lens. For example, children are taught during their early stages that no one should know what happens at home out of fear that they can be taken away. "What happens here, stays here" is a fear-based response to historical traumas imposed by biased systems.

Surviving in these systems is simply exhausting. The battle can definitely feel uphill and never-ending. Understanding the historical roots that create this battle is important and allows us to become intentional about how we move in this world. A part of reclaiming and rewriting our narrative is understanding how the script was set up to begin with. Racial injustice and systemic inequality originated before the days of slavery and are baked into every aspect of how the United States operates. For many, this reality continues to go unacknowledged, as seen in debates related to police reform, changing school curriculums, or advocating for culturally informed health-care practices. Racial injustice and systemic inequality have many layers, and it takes intentionality and consistent work to recognize and undo them.

Furthermore, movements that center racial identities, such as the "Black Lives Matter" movement, also fail to give space to the unique experiences of Black women, as they center Black men instead.

# Unpacking Inherited Trauma

We take many things from our ancestors and those who have come before us, like our grandmother's hips or the stories passed down from our great-grandfathers. Many of us formulate our values and beliefs from who and what we come from. It is important to know that our own history and context shape who we are today.

We take many great aspects from our ancestors—resilience, culture, and joy, to name just a few. We also carry many years of unresolved hurt, pain, and anger. As a community of people who have had to survive for years, many of those survival behaviors have been passed on through generations. And now here you are today. Full of that same resilience, culture, and joy, but also the hurt, pain, and anger passed down as well.

Our ancestors influence who we are since birth. The very day you came into this world, you were born with all this "stuff." Some of this stuff is trapped in your body. Literally. We know that stress can change the physical makeup of our cells. According to a clinical article published by Zur Institute on "Understanding and Treating Intergenerational Transmission of Trauma," traumatic experiences—such as slavery—can be transmitted physiologically, environmentally, and socially. Some of the things we carry today are not our own. In order to truly heal, we must process and release this "stuff."

Take a moment to think about some of the "stuff" you may be holding on to that is not your own. I'll even give you some starters to get you thinking. Do you resonate with "having to work ten times harder"? Do you feel the need to take care of everyone around you but yourself? Do you parent to teach your children to survive? All of these concepts are influenced by the history and context of our ancestors. I encourage you to lean deeper into the "stuff" you may carry from your ancestors. Why does it exist? Could it be survival? Are you trying to make it through the day with everyone you care about safe, alive, and healthy? Whether it's that you're just trying to survive day by day or something else, let's move from survival to healing.

Jenesis is a twenty-one-year-old Black woman who is going to school to become a physical therapist. Much of Jenesis's childhood was spent in her hometown. She never traveled much outside her neighborhood and has had many of her same friends all her life. It is now, during Jenesis's studies, that she has become more aware of her identity as a Black woman. She begins noticing how her male counterparts often cut her off when she is speaking and fail to consider her point of view. She is starting to see the disparities in medical care among the Black-women patients her student clinic serves.

More recently, she has been watching news coverage related to the death of an unarmed Black person in the midst of police brutality. Jenesis feels overwhelmed and hasn't been getting much sleep. When she vents to her friends and family, they don't usually offer anything more than "You are strong" or "You'll be okay." She wants to tell them more but fears that she'll be seen as weak or a burden.

All of these things have impacted Jenesis's view of herself. Sometimes she wonders, "Is this how I am supposed to feel?" And at the core, Jenesis wonders if she's even worth anything else. One day Jenesis became so overwhelmed, she broke out into tears during class. Her professor recommended a support group for Black women in her area. With the assistance of this group, Jenesis is beginning to understand that she is not alone in these feelings, and she has begun to unpack some of these stressors in a healthy way by incorporating meditation, deep breathing, and weekly check-ins with her community.

# When Feelings of Shame Turn Inward

Shame is a familiar feeling that often lives within Black women. Much of it stems from the consistent policing of our behavior. As the world tries to force us into a box, many of us have learned to internalize this shame or start to believe it's justified. Imagine shame as a voice telling us that we do not fit in, that we are not good enough, or that we are "doing too much." It's one thing when these messages come from specific people or society in general, but imagine this voice being your own. This is how internalized shame works.

A part of releasing shame is managing our own expectations. We may feel shame about not being a perfect mother or partner. We might feel shame about our bodies and how we dress. We may feel shame about where we come from and the resources we didn't have. Shame can also be present in the way we interact with other Black women—consider the ways you may police other Black women's bodies, hair, or mannerisms. Sometimes we are guilty of policing our sisters, too. Although shame lives within all of us, it's up to us to decide how loud that voice will be.

Controlling the volume of that inner voice can be challenging at first, but it's important to first bring awareness to your shame and simply call it what it is. Often, shame can hide behind feelings of sadness and anger, but even when those feelings disappear, shame still sticks around. Shame often manifests as negative self-talk. Paying close attention to these behaviors will assist in your volume control.

# The Effects of Racial Microaggressions

A microaggression is an act, sometimes subtle, that reflects stereotypes and results in harm or offense to a marginalized group. It's important to note that microaggressions can be overt or covert and may or may not be intentional. Nonetheless, they are harmful to whomever they are directed at. For our purposes, the type of harmful act we're focusing on is racial microaggression. For Black women specifically, some of the common microaggressions hold "whiteness" or respectability politics as the standard, insinuating that anything less is incorrect. As the name insinuates, sometimes microaggressions are seen as small acts of prejudice or discrimination, but the impact can still be great.

Black women often have a hard time processing microaggressions for two main reasons: (1) not wanting to be seen as confrontational and having that misconstrued as aggression and (2) fear of being gaslit or having to take on the additional role or being a caretaker or educator. And so, many Black women tolerate these frequent assaults, believing they have to. But over time, you learn to adapt to these tiny assaults and begin believing that what's being said and done is actually true. That you are inherently aggressive or unprofessional.

Let's unpack a few of the following common microaggressions.

## TONE POLICING

Comments directed at the way we speak or our tone of voice can include: "You are so articulate," "You speak English very well," "You don't have to get loud and ghetto," or any implication that the use of Ebonics and African American Vernacular English (AAVE) is incorrect. The underlying assumption here is that Black women are inherently unintelligent and loud. This can lead to us feeling the need to overcompensate for intelligence and/or feel self-conscious about expressing our emotions and ideas confidently. One of the consequences of this is that Black women will feel like they can't safely express themselves. It is another way to silence them.

## TOUCHING OR COMMENTING ON HAIR

Physical advances or comments directed at our hair can look like the following: "OMG, how did you get your hair to do that? Can I touch it?" Or comments such as "Wow, it looks so wild and crazy." The underlying basis of these comments insinuate that Black women have unruly, untamed hair or exoticize our features, as if they are out of the norm. These comments can also come from men, more likely expressing their hierarchy of desirability. Furthermore, anyone trying to touch your hair or body without your permission violates your personal boundaries or simply implies you don't have any. This further dehumanizes Black women—leading us back to a struggle of self-worth.

## APPEARANCE POLICING/DOUBLE STANDARDS

Insinuations that our hairstyles and outfits are inappropriate or unprofessional are too common. Often, these prejudices are even infused in work and school policies as means to police us. This can look like wearing the same pencil skirt to work as your white colleague, but yours being seen as "provocative." This can lead to us being hypervigilant about our appearances and bodies. It also encourages us to deny pieces of ourselves in an effort to conform.

## COMMENTS ON BEAUTY

Sometimes people will make comments that rank attractiveness and desirability. This can sound like "You're pretty for a dark-skinned girl," "She has that good hair," or even statements that exoticize Black women—such as "the blacker the berry, the sweeter the juice." These kinds of microaggressions imply a hierarchy of value based on physical attributes. It also tells Black women that their inherent worth rests in things such as skin color, hair texture, or sexual performance. These comments, especially from men, are rooted in white patriarchal standards of beauty.

## DISRESPECTING NAMES

Intentionally mispronouncing someone's name or not taking the time to pronounce it correctly can be harmful. Even more so, categorizing names as "ghetto" or "ratchet" can be equally damaging. This can look like referring to all Black women as an "Alize" or "Shenanah." The more common consequence to this is Black women feeling like our names—which are a part of our cultural identities—are too "complicated" or unacceptable. Many Black women have learned to shorten their name or go by a nickname for convenience and ease, but that can result in self-hatred or identity erasure. Imagine the implications of telling a young Black girl that the one thing meant to identify her and set her apart is too complicated or "ghetto."

## ASSUMING AGGRESSION

Another microaggression is perceiving encounters with Black women as aggressive. This can show up in interpersonal relationships with Black men, whether romantic or not, or in casual interactions with strangers. It holds the basis that Black women are always angry and aggressive and plays into the stereotype of the "angry Black woman." Being unable to be seen as soft and vulnerable further dehumanizes our experiences as Black women. We are often forced to internalize normal reactions of anger or sadness for fear of being perceived as aggressive.

# Knowing and Loving Who You Are

There are many lived experiences in the world today that threaten how we view and love ourselves. As we continue to unpack these things, it's important to remain grounded in how you choose to show up in this world. Deeply consider who you are and who you wish to be. I challenge you to begin removing the filters placed by this world as you move along this self-love journey. Learning the ways you wish to love yourself will help teach those around you how you are meant to be loved. Teach them to say your name slowly and accurately. Teach them to respect your physical space and boundaries. Teach them that you can be soft and assertive. Teach them that you are human and more than just your hair and body.

## KEY TAKEAWAYS

**W**e have taken a surface-level look at many shared experiences of Black women today, in an effort to set the scene and briefly explore some context and history.

- As Black women, our inherent power is limitless; however, there are many systems set up to limit us.

- The stereotype of the "strong Black woman" can dehumanize Black women.

- Being a Black woman encompasses two marginalized identities that are sometimes tough to navigate.

- Racial injustice and systemic inequality are real and live at the core of self-love issues for Black women.

- Healing is layered and requires an intergenerational look into the "stuff" we carry today.

# CHAPTER 2

# UNDERSTANDING SELF-LOVE

am happy you made it here! In this next section, we will begin to explore the concept of "self-love." We will walk through what self-love is—feeling worthy; what it may look like—taking care of yourself; some misconceptions about what self-love is—being perfect and flawless; and how powerful it can be when incorporated into our lives—having healthy and joyful relationships. We'll also talk about how the way we view and love ourselves can improve our lives for the better. Let's begin!

# Defining Self-Love

Self-love at its core can be defined as "the belief you hold that you are a valuable and worthy person." Before you can love, care for, or appreciate someone or something else, you must first recognize that the person or thing has inherent value and worth. And once you recognize your value and worth, you must practice feeding your newly found recognition. A self-love practice lies in the concept that you still love yourself, even if perfection, happiness, or success don't feel attainable. Our self-love practices should all lead back to the concept that we are worthy of love, joy, and happiness, and we don't have to earn that worth. This can look like viewing yourself in a positive light and being confident in who you are—don't worry sis, if you struggle with this now, I will provide some guidance later in this workbook. We will continue to explore ways to develop or enhance our self-love practices.

# What Self-Love Is Not

It's important to note that self-love should *not* be rooted in trying to be perfect or in how productive we are. Sometimes we view self-love practices as a magical land where everyone is always happy, successful, and carefree. Unfortunately, this is a myth.

Self-love is also not rooted in the things we can do for *others*. As Black women, we assume a caretaking role for many—however, our worth should not be determined by what we can or cannot do for others.

Finally, self-love is both a destination and a journey. As with many healing journeys, there is no absolute finish line; however, you can be grounded in the concept of self-love. Referring back to this road will help you when you go astray. Life happens and at different stages of your life, your self-love practices may look different, but being grounded in your worth and value (i.e., positive self-talk, boundary setting, and self-care) will help lead the way on any path you take.

Melanie is a thirty-two-year-old Black woman engaging in therapy. Throughout her sessions, Melanie has been challenged to set boundaries with her friends and family members. Melanie has discussed feeling like she always has to be there for those around her and feels like they always expect her to show up for them, even at her own expense. Melanie has often discussed skipping out on the things she wanted and needed to do for herself in order to help a friend.

Although Melanie has identified the need to set boundaries and now has the skills to do so, she still has experienced some doubt. Melanie places her phone on silent after a certain hour at night, schedules time for herself, and is able to communicate her priorities to those close to her. Upon further processing, Melanie has discovered that she has tied her self-worth to her ability to provide for others. She now has to learn new ways to affirm her self-worth by developing a solid self-love practice that centers her. Melanie is working on affirmations like "I am more than what I can do for others."

# Whew Chile, It's a Struggle: Self-Love Is Simple but Sometimes Tough

Self-love may seem like a very straightforward and simple concept. Just believe in our own worth and value. Sounds like a piece of cake, right? It becomes difficult because there are so many filters and systems that have devalued us and lessened our worth or taught us to tie our worth and value to what we do for others, just like Melanie. Furthermore, the many other areas of one's identity—including sexuality and ability status—may further complicate this journey. In the case study above, sis was challenged to set boundaries (one of the best self-love practices) but came out feeling empty. A true self-love journey may require us to unlearn behaviors, relearn who we are without the world's filters, and pour back into ourselves all the love that we give so freely to everyone else. And that, Family, is the "work"—self-love in practice.

Here are a few steps that can help turn the concept of self-love into a practice that is tailor-made just for you:

## EXAMINE INSECURITIES

Take time for introspection to understand your own insecurities and fears. Ask yourself: Who might I be without the filters of this world? This may look like acknowledging the current behaviors and thoughts you carry and assessing if they truly serve your goal of self-love.

## RECALIBRATE EXPECTATIONS

Let go of perfection. Accountability is fine and necessary, but consistently trying to obtain an unrealistic standard will give power to a voice saying "you'll never be good enough." This may look like offering yourself grace and flexibility in your journey—think "it's okay to just be okay."

## PRIORITIZE YOURSELF

Don't confuse selfishness with self-preservation. There are many times where it is necessary to put ourselves first. Consider the ways you will pour into yourself just because you can. This may look like being intentional about what you eat or taking fifteen-minute "brain breaks" throughout your day.

Get a firm grip on what grounds you in this world. What are your values and beliefs? This may include unlearning or letting go of beliefs that you were taught. Consider who you truly are, what you like, and what you really want.

# Self-Love and Relationships

The ways we interact with ourselves influence how we interact with others. In our case study earlier, we met a sister, Melanie, who spent most of her life pouring her energy into those around her. This was fulfilling for her in some ways, but still left her feeling empty and, in some instances, resentful. Sound familiar? Many women are taught that what we put into our relationships will reflect our worth and what we deserve. But instead, we should look at it through a different lens. Our ability to give and put into our relationships should be seen as a reflection of what we give and put into ourselves. We are worthy of love, joy, and happiness—period. And what we choose to give to others should not compromise our worthiness and what we deserve.

No matter how strong we think our mask—or performance of perfectionism—may be, if we are not grounded in self-love, our interactions with others can be negatively impacted. Our self-image affects how we allow people to treat us, the expectations we place on our children, and even how we show up at work. It can look like a spirit of perfectionism or competition. It can even look like bullying or self-doubt. For example, a mask that Black women often wear is the need to be "professional," poised, and hardworking. A person who wears this mask consistently may find that they are given more tedious tasks in the workplace because others feel they can "handle it." That person may also have high expectations of their children and may be seen as controlling or strict. And finally, this person may feel consistent pressure to overperform—which can lead to competitiveness with others—and have deep bouts of depression or anxiety when they are unable to complete tasks perfectly.

Let's take a moment to reflect on how low self-esteem or a lack or self-love may have impacted our past relationships. Keep this in the back of your mind as we move throughout the workbook.

## PAYING ATTENTION TO SELF-LOVE (WAITING TO EXHALE)

Take a moment to refocus your attention back to you. Consider your self-love practice a journey to return home. It's within you where you should remain grounded and steady, no matter what's happening around you. Take this moment to embrace yourself with a hug. Take a deep breath. As you inhale, squeeze yourself tightly and slowly release upon exhale. Do this as many times as you need to feel grounded back to yourself ... back at home.

How did you feel before doing this practice? How did you feel afterward? If this was helpful, keep it in mind for times you're feeling overwhelmed or disconnected from yourself.

## The Pursuit of Happiness

Although there is no one final destination on this self-love journey, the farther you travel, the more time you will spend in a state of true happiness. Being able to turn back to yourself, no matter what's happening around you, and find joy is a kind of peace you can't buy. There is freedom in this journey—letting go of self-doubt, fear, feeling unworthy, and self-criticism creates space to imagine, grow, and heal. You have taken the first several steps to begin this journey. It's important to note that these practices are to identify and focus on the areas you can control. We cannot change the world we live in, but we can continue to pour into ourselves, remove filters and masks, and build upon our peace of mind. Soon, you won't allow many things into your life that don't align with your values, beliefs, and self-love mission.

# Making Yourself the Priority

As we alluded to earlier, your self-love journey has to be rooted in you. It is necessary to prioritize yourself. Remember, self-preservation is not the same as selfishness. For Black women who have been taught that their worth is measured by what we can do for others—this will be a challenge. It requires having real, raw, and honest conversations with yourself and those who have benefitted from your lack of self-love. Boundary work is healing work. Expect resistance and maybe even some shame and guilt. We will explore later what to do with those feelings. This journey may require navigating your own internal resistance, as well as others learning to readjust to a different version of you. The risk in not putting your happiness and fulfillment first is emptiness. Sure, there is fulfillment in doing for others, raising children, and putting energy into a job, but all of those things have an ending point. The fulfillment is temporary and often does not stand the test of time. When you are grounded in a self-love practice, it takes a lot less energy to find fulfillment, peace, joy, and happiness.

# There's No Time Like the Present

The time is now. There's no better moment to reconnect with yourself and strengthen your foundation. It's possible that it doesn't "feel" like the best time for you to center yourself. Too many things going on right now . . . or you may be telling yourself, "I'll just wait until . . ." Remember, there is risk in not putting your happiness and fulfillment first. What's great is that you don't need to pay a co-pay or find a babysitter. You don't have to buy any fancy journals or special gel pens. All you need is something to write with, a safe and comfortable space, and an open mind. Here are a few things to consider as you begin this self-love journey.

### BE GENTLE WITH YOURSELF

Grace and compassion are among the highest forms of self-love. Be sure to honor how you feel throughout these pages. It's important to say "ouch" when something hurts because then you validate that it's there. Remember to go to the edge of your comfort zone, but always respect your limitations. Discerning being uncomfortable versus feeling threatened is a valuable skill.

## BE PATIENT AND PRACTICAL

Now is a good time to practice letting go of expectations of perfection. There is no race in this journey; in fact, taking your time and being very intentional can only make your foundation stronger. Consider it like taking the scenic route on this journey, because the growth is in the *process*, not the *product*. You will not change the way you think or act overnight. Unlearning harmful behaviors and relearning new ones can be painful and difficult. Be patient, practical, and present.

## ELEVATING YOUR ENVIRONMENT

Embracing flow and growth requires intentionality and shifting your status quo. What might it look like for you to have a physical space that mirrors your journey? One that affirms you, your mistakes, and room to flourish? For my neurodivergent folks or those who may feel pressure to do what you feel you're "supposed" to do, how might it feel to create a space that fits *your* needs and not those of everyone else? Now consider creating a mental space that also affirms your process. This may include bringing in accountability partners and stating your commitment of self-love to yourself daily. Accountability partners are meant to be people in your social network who are also committed to or value the same cause. Accountability partners are generally used for motivation and check-ins along the journey. You may find time to work on this workbook together or outline goals to check in on at different points. When considering an accountability partner, be sure their self-love mission is in alignment with yours and that they are able to offer nonjudgmental support in the ways you need.

# KEY TAKEAWAYS

**A**s we have discussed, self-love is a journey. Sometimes that journey feels more like a marathon than a sprint, but we know that there is reward in pressing on. Here are some key takeaways:

- Our self-love practices should all lead back to the concept that we are inherently worthy and we don't have to earn that worth.

- Self-love should *not* be rooted in being perfect or in the ways we can produce.

- A true self-love journey may require us to unlearn behaviors and relearn who we are without the world's filters.

- When you have a foundation of self-love, you begin to be more intentional in all areas of your life.

# CHAPTER 3

# PRACTICING SELF-LOVE AS A BLACK WOMAN

Happy to see you're still sticking around! In this next section, we will explore what it looks like and why it's so important to practice self-love as a Black woman. Self-love is the road to nurturing and empowering our inner goddess. With that being said, there are many things in this world that we don't have control over. I know that you can't self-love yourself out of racism, sexism, discrimination, or any other form of oppression. It's in the face of these much bigger and more complex issues that I encourage my clients to focus on the ways we do have power. And so, I encourage you, too. There are many things you *can* control—taking this journey to self-love is one of them.

# Understanding and Identifying Your Feelings

One of the necessary steps on this self-love journey is identifying and understanding your emotions. Our emotions drive our thoughts, and our thoughts drive our actions, and this can be an ongoing cycle. If our emotions are negative, this drives negative thoughts and then negative actions, and nothing will ever change. That means we must do something different. In order to do something different, we have to address those underlying emotions. Next, I have briefly outlined simple ways to practice this fundamental skill. Remember that skill-building may take time and practice.

## NAMING YOUR FEELINGS

In the world of therapy, we like to use the concept "name it to tame it"—to help individuals begin to recognize and control their feelings. Emotional identification is a skill that may take some practice to develop. Often people limit their feelings to a handful of descriptors—mad, sad, happy, or "fine." These do not adequately describe the complexity of feelings we are capable of. I encourage everyone to look up a wheel of emotions or "feelings wheel" to broaden your language and assist with emotional identification. You can find a user-friendly one on feelingswheel.com—pretty convenient, right? Use this tool when you feel you are unable to adequately express yourself or even to understand how many more feeling descriptors exist.

## BEING MINDFUL OF YOUR FEELINGS

After you are able to name your feelings, you'll need to sharpen your ability to recognize when they are coming up for you. This can go something like "I recognize that I am becoming impatient and easily agitated; I may be feeling anxious at this moment."

It's also important to consider how your feelings influence your actions. This can go something like "I recognize that I am becoming impatient and easily agitated—when I become anxious, I am more likely to perceive things as a threat, which leads to me being argumentative." Consider: When you're sad, are you more likely to isolate? When you feel unsafe, does it come out as anger? When you feel insecure, are you more likely to engage in negative self-talk?

Being mindful of your feelings allows you to be more present and intentional about what you do with those feelings. We are not at a stage to process or shift these feelings yet; we are simply flexing our muscles of understanding and identifying our emotions.

## ACCEPTING YOUR FEELINGS

Becoming comfortable with your feelings—all your feelings—is key. Often-times we either avoid or suppress the emotions that don't make us feel great. But when we are uncomfortable with our feelings, we are allowing them to control us. The goal is for us to be in the driver's seat. Recognizing and then accepting our feelings is another stop on our self-love journey, allowing us to remain level-headed and permitting us to better control our reactions. Stay tuned for an activity related to emotional identification.

# Reaching for Self-Love

Sometimes it's difficult to take a journey if you don't know the destination. Many people don't even know what it looks like to love themselves. As with many people, we are more likely to focus on the negative. Now, let's start where we are. Consider the things you do or say to yourself that don't serve your highest self—and work forward. For example, someone may know that they are not satisfied with the way they speak to themselves or how they view their body. It may not be easy to conceptualize what self-love overall looks like, but they could use these two points to begin. They may wish to speak to themselves more kindly and to love their body unconditionally. These become destinations on their journey to self-love. So now, instead of focusing on a grand view of self-love, this person could pull their attention to those two destinations. This can create a solid definition of their version of self-love.

Remember, this journey will not be easy and will take work, but know that you are not doing it alone. Here are some ways to stay grounded during this journey.

I have worked with a young woman for several years, Akela. Akela is a "kitchen beautician" or home hairstylist, on the road to owning her own business. Akela is a survivor of a domestic violence relationship that happened years ago. She has since moved on and has found herself in a relatively safe and healthy relationship. During our sessions, Akela has often talked about how her current partner's natural tendency to be submissive was extremely aggravating for her. As we sat with Akela's initial feeling of "aggravation," we uncovered that her partner's submissive behavior reminded her of the loss of power she experienced years ago in her previous relationship. Akela was triggered and found herself placing some internalized shame into her relationship.

Using this level of awareness, Akela has been able to identify when her feelings of "aggravation" are likely to lead to conflict in her relationship. Akela continues to work on processing her feelings and has seen positive outcomes in feeling closer to her partner. Her ability to work alongside her feelings gives her back some of those pieces of power and control that once were taken away. Akela is more open, intimate, and in tune with herself, which allows her to be the same with her partner. Remember, the work you do individually can only lead to better and healthier relationships. You are worthy of better and healthier relationships.

## IT'S A SIGN OF STRENGTH TO BE VULNERABLE

When I first began my self-love journey, I used to think feeling my feelings, crying, and opening up were all signs of weakness. However, I used to admire and even envy those who did. After all, it wouldn't be great to carry this train of thought into the therapy room because if this is what I thought of myself, then what did I think about my clients? Recognizing vulnerability as a strength was a pivotal moment in my self-love journey. Think about it: it's much easier to do what makes us more comfortable—to avoid and suppress. It requires a lot of strength and courage to move out of that comfort zone. Vulnerability is the catalyst that allows you to be honest with yourself and those around you. Consider vulnerability as the space you must enter in order to truly grow and change.

## TAKE YOUR TIME AND YOU'LL SEE RESULTS

All good things take time. This may seem cliché, but it couldn't be truer when speaking of self-love. The more intentional you are, the more you will learn about yourself. The power is truly in the process and not the product. As you and those around you meet the healing versions of yourself, new challenges will arise. Putting in the time to work through these strategies and exercises will get you closer and closer to those self-love goals.

## HONESTY IS THE ONLY WAY

Self-love means loving you and all your parts—even the ones you'd rather not acknowledge. Honesty and transparency are critical to the sustainability and longevity of this work. Real change cannot come from dishonesty. A famous philosopher, Aubrey "Drake" Graham, discussed the idea of no fake love—are you the "fake friend" showing "fake love" to yourself? This can be a slow and/or painful process—it takes time, but I encourage you to stay the course. Be real with yourself.

## PUT YOURSELF FIRST

If you like it, you should put a ring on it . . . if you love it, you should put it first. It's in this act that you communicate your commitment to yourself and your healing journey. You cannot pour from an empty cup. Putting yourself

# CREATE BOUNDARIES TO
# SUPPORT SELF-LOVE

"Boundary work is healing work"—I live by this saying. Boundaries are a fundamental piece to this healing stuff. Boundaries are the buffers we put in place to protect our physical, emotional, and mental wants and needs. Many Black women struggle to set and follow through with boundaries, and then we find ourselves exhausted, taken advantage of, and, in some cases, abused and mistreated. A lot of the barriers that come with setting boundaries lie in the way we view them. Many of us were taught that setting boundaries as children was a means of challenging authority. A good example of this is expressing that you didn't like or want to do something—like not wanting to hug or talk to family member. We may have received messages back that we are to do as we are told or expected, no matter what we truly want or feel, simply because someone "said so." We received messages that we did not have personal autonomy. Instead of thinking of boundaries as saying no to others, consider them as saying yes to yourself. Many times, we go along with things in an attempt to "keep the peace"—but what about the internal turmoil it causes you? Is it peaceful there?

first is one the most important steps to achieving self-love. Getting to a place where you feel worthy enough to be one of the priorities in your life is groundbreaking. For some, this may feel counterintuitive—the socialization of Black women to be caretakers and neglect our own needs has a strong grip. Please know that you are not alone—there's a community of women working through this same struggle to loosen that grip.

## How to Cultivate Self-Love

To cultivate means to develop or grow. It's important for me to continually stress that self-love is a process. A beautiful but messy journey. The messy pieces of this journey include moments of self-accountability, radical acceptance, and pushing through some of the pain and fear we have known for so long. The activities in this workbook will equip you with the necessary tools to give you strength on this journey. The beauty in the journey is learning about yourself in new ways, strengthening the relationship you have with yourself, and beginning to incorporate joy and grace into how you wish to show up in this world. The following tools can stick with you as you navigate.

### BECOME MINDFUL

The most boiled-down definition of mindfulness is a state of being consciously aware of something, without judgment. Some achieve this through meditation or breath work. It can also look like intentional awareness in everyday activities like eating, showering, or walking. The goal isn't to be a blank canvas and to achieve absolute stillness but instead to slow things down for better control and awareness. Let's practice right now, in this moment. Take a big, deep breath and note the following: What does your body feel like right now? Does it feel heavy or light? Is there any pain or discomfort? What are some things you can smell in this moment? Are the smells pleasant? Do they bring an emotional response? Notice that these questions didn't ask you change anything or do anything differently—they simply bring awareness. Being mindful or present is incredibly important but may take some practice. Oftentimes we get wrapped up in school, work, and caretaking and miss out on the opportunity to just "pause."

## ACT ON WHAT YOU NEED

Fulfilling our needs doesn't have to be inconvenient or laborious. In fact, the more we tend to our physical, mental, and emotional needs, the easier it will get. Consider it like car maintenance. If you get regular oil changes, check the tire pressure, and rotate your tires, the less likely you are to have a major expense down the line. And just like keeping up with your car's maintenance schedule in increments, it's important to also compartmentalize your needs into mind, body, and spirit, all of which we will explore later in the workbook.

## PRACTICE GOOD SELF-CARE

As a reminder, self-care is not selfish. Self-care shouldn't be performative, either. It's okay to share pictures of your bubble bath or invite a friend to dinner, but be intentional to redirect your self-care energy back into you. A tip for making self-care sustainable is to infuse it into your day-to-day activities. Now you may be thinking, "Lady, I struggle to do self-care, period—how I am supposed to do it daily?" Don't worry, sis, I got you in just a bit.

## SET BOUNDARIES

Boundaries are ways to communicate your values and beliefs. They teach others how to love you. Most of all, setting boundaries is an act of alignment. If you say that you want to attract healthy relationships, boundary work says you can't align with or allow unhealthy behaviors. For many, we view boundaries as a negative—what we don't want. Instead focus on what you are communicating. What *do* you want?

## FORGIVE YOURSELF

Besides boundary setting, the most difficult piece of this journey we may struggle with is forgiveness. We are often able to give compassion to others above ourselves. In order to step into a new chapter, we must release any weight we are carrying. Release the guilt and shame about ourselves and our past behaviors. We deserve relationships that are grounded in the idea of "rupture and repair," and this first needs to be modeled with ourselves. Rupture and repair is the notion of acknowledging that we will not always be perfect and we will cause harm at some point, but focusing our efforts on repair is necessary. This concept is originally derived from studying attachment with babies, but it is very much applicable for adults, too. Both groups have needs we want met and struggle to communicate that effectively. Please note that it is possible to be forgiving and still take responsibility and accountability for our actions and how those actions have impacted others.

## LIVE WITH INTENTION

Living life on autopilot is so easy. Am I right? Wake up, go to work, care for the kids, make dinner, go to sleep, and do it all over again. Living life with intention is like asking yourself, "What is it that I wish to get out of this moment?" and then aligning your actions with that. We have lived in survival mode long enough. In this chapter of our lives, let's be intentional.

# Letting Go Is Hard but Necessary

In order to welcome new ideas, people, or things into our life, releasing the stuff that doesn't align is imperative. We have to make room for this new version of ourselves to emerge. Change can be scary. If we continue to look at letting go with a fear-based mindset, we will continue to face barriers preventing us from obtaining what we desire. Releasing the stuff that doesn't serve is an act of self-love. I know that the fear of letting go can be intimidating, but holding on will only block us from moving into where we should be: a place of love, well-being, self-fulfillment, and happiness.

# Don't Be Afraid to Ask for Help

As mentioned earlier, the disparities that exist with Black women's health—both mentally and physically—are jarring. The statistics showing the low number of Black women who are offered or seek help is one reason these disparities not only still exist but continue to grow. An article published in the *Journal of Black Psychology*, "Do I Really Need to Go and See Somebody? Black Women's Perceptions of Help-Seeking for Depression," notes that Black women often delay seeking treatment until symptoms are severe. There may be many reasons why some Black women do not seek help. Perhaps it's a lack of resources (social capital, money, knowledge, etc.), lack of trust (in clinicians, medical staff, or other community supports), or a stigma about receiving services. It could be anything. I encourage you to think about whether you struggle to ask for help. If so, what are the reasons why you hesitate? Are you afraid that you will be viewed as weak? Are you hesitant about becoming a burden to others? Do you know how to identify when/if you need help? As we discuss goals for self-love, consider adding "asking for help." There are many platforms and resources that exist to combat these things, some of which are included in the Resources section at the end of this book (see page 154).

A part of self-love is feeling worthy enough to have a community. You deserve a safe, reliable, and helpful community. Many of us don't want to burden others with our issues. When we feel we've become a burden, we eliminate the opportunity for others to show up for us. Maybe you have asked for help in the past and it didn't work out . . . I'm sure that was hurtful. I'm sure it made you never want to reach out again. But it's time to move forward. It's your responsibility to get the help you need and communicate *how* you need it. We have been silenced as Black women, conditioned to not feel worthy of asking for help. It's time to reclaim our voices.

# KEY TAKEAWAYS

In this chapter, we explored what it may look like to practice self-love as a Black woman. There are many detours on this journey, but it's important to take your time with each new practice. Remember to extend yourself grace and patience. Know that you are not alone in this journey. Black women are loving themselves, and I am here for it! Here are some key points to keep in mind:

- Being in the driver's seat of your emotions is key. In order to accomplish this goal, you must name your feelings, be mindful of your feelings, and accept those feelings.

- It is a sign of strength to be vulnerable. I encourage you to see vulnerability as the space for healing and growth.

- Boundary work is healing work. Part of our obstacles with setting boundaries present in the way we view them. Boundaries teach others how to love you and communicate to yourself what you will not accept.

- Letting go is scary, but it's important to move away from allowing fear to drive your decisions. Moving things out of the way creates space for new things to enter.

- You deserve a safe, reliable, and helpful community. Asking for help when you need it lets you reclaim your voice.

# PART II

# PUTTING SELF-LOVE INTO PRACTICE

You made it so far, mama! I am so excited to begin walking through a series of exercises, affirmations, practices, and strategies aimed at the various elements of self-love . . . just for you! These exercises will help you make room for positive change, new beliefs, and healthier actions. The goal is to reach a point where you love and accept yourself with ease. A point where you realize no matter the weather, if your journey is full of sunny days or storms, your foundation will remain strong and steady through it all.

# CHAPTER 4

# LOVE WHERE YOU ARE

This section will begin to help you determine where you are in your self-love journey and where you may need to focus (or pour in) some energy. It's important to note that no matter where you are and where you want to be, you can find self-love along the entire journey. Working on yourself and loving yourself can happen at the same time. While self-love is about acceptance, it is also about growing into a better version of yourself. In this section, you'll work on setting some manageable goals that you want to achieve in your journey and incorporating them into your life so that you can find success with them. Feel free to revisit these activities and affirmations at any time to see what may have shifted and what may need to be revisited and modified to fit a new goal that better suits you.

**M**any of my clients have a hard time slowing down and taking the temperature on where they are in their current self-love journey. This was no different for thirty-five-year-old Oya. Oya was so determined to do a complete 180 and transform into a new person. She wanted to change how she dressed; she wished she could walk into every space without a doubt; she wanted to be unapologetically authentic. She has often referred to her journey as becoming "that girl." One of the biggest challenges that Oya faced was slowing down and being present. Using some of the exercises in this workbook, Oya began to realize that where she was in her journey gave her more answers on how to get where she wanted to go. She also developed compassion and appreciation for who she was and the path she took to get there. It's true that she wanted to be more confident in spaces like work and school, but she also found appreciation for how she showed up in her personal relationships. She reflected on how her style continues to shift and grow alongside her season of self-exploration. She discovered that she was authentic in her beliefs and values and just needed to focus her energy on standing her ground consistently. Oya has realized that she has always been "that girl" and she should refocus her energy on pouring into who she already was.

# I AM ENOUGH,
# EXACTLY AS I AM.

## EXERCISE | **SELF-LOVE ASSESSMENT: START WHERE YOU ARE**

The first step in your self-love journey is taking stock of how you feel about yourself now. There are no right or wrong answers; this assessment will identify areas you might want to focus on. Revisit this assessment when you're done with the workbook and note if any of your answers have changed.

Here is a list of possible beliefs we can have about ourselves that reflect self-love, self-confidence, and self-worth. Check off the statements that are true for you.

☐ I love my hair as it is.

☐ I love every part of my body.

☐ I am a good friend.

☐ I deserve good things.

☐ I have a positive relationship with money.

☐ I show up as myself at work or school.

☐ I attract relationships that are positive and healthy.

☐ I am where I want to be in life.

☐ I practice self-care frequently.

☐ I am more than what I can do for others.

PROMPT | Think about the things you already do that communicate love to yourself. Which of these are most effective? How can you enhance or build on these practices?

## EXERCISE | **UNMASK: FACING THE HIDDEN TRUTH**

Recall that in part 1, we discussed the masks Black women wear in this world. In this exercise we will begin to unpack our dual identities. Many Black women have two "faces"—the one we show everyone else and the one we wear when we're alone. The one we show everyone else is a mask—one we put on every morning even when we barely have the energy. This mask hides our insecurities, trauma, pain, and fears.

Using the following two basic outlines, describe what attributes you present to the world versus the ones you to keep hidden. Fill in each face with words, phrases, and/or images that represent your two sides and label each face.

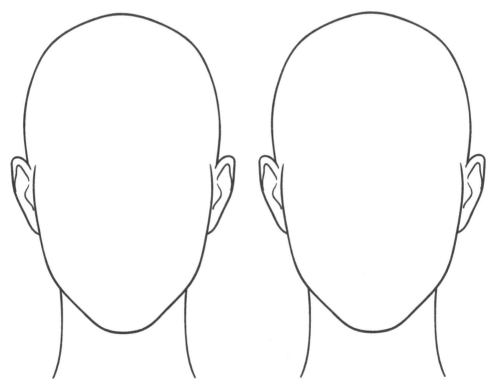

PROMPT | The way we view things is heavily influenced by our environment and the values of society. It is important to identify these ideas and figure out what pieces we wish to keep and what we would like to let go of. What negative messages about your physical appearance (body, hair, skin complexion, weight, etc.) did you receive growing up? How did these messages influence how you cared for your body? What pieces would you like to let go of or shift?

## PRACTICE | **BODY-ODY APPRECIATION: MIRROR WORK**

Many women struggle to love themselves unconditionally when they look into the mirror—so they just don't. This is an activity to love each piece of you, as you are, in this exact moment.

Looking into the mirror, you are going to touch every part of your body and say out loud why you are grateful for it. For example, "I am grateful for my tummy, as it is, because it lets me know when I am hungry and need to take care of myself." Or, "I am grateful for my hair because it is my crown and can be used to express my creative nature." It's very important to take your time and embrace each body part as you proclaim your gratefulness. You can do this activity every morning or night, as well as when you start to hear that negative self-talk related to your body image.

**BUILDING OUR ARMOR**

You can be as strong and graceful as Wonder Woman, but she has a shield for a reason. No matter how strong you are, you are not invincible. There will be plenty of things in this world that will threaten your self-love. This activity will help equip you with armor to deflect harm.

In the space provided, write the gifts, talents, and positive traits you already hold. This could be something like using humor to cope or being a good writer. You will continue to build upon these gifts, talents, and positive traits in the next several sections.

PROMPT | Think about the women in your family or the women you have grown up with—across generations. Write a letter to them. Begin it with "To the women of the _____ family." Write to those you know and those you may not have had the chance to meet. What are the things you are grateful for? What do you wish you could let go of? Think about the women who will come after you. What is your wish for them?

# ACCEPTING COMPLIMENTS

Very often Black women struggle to accept compliments about themselves. Part of that is because we don't truly believe in the words being said. It is possible to love and believe good things about ourselves and still be humble. This exercise will make us more intentional about our view of ourselves and how we interact with others.

When you receive compliments from both strangers and people familiar to you, practice using the phrase "I accept that, thank you." As you do this, pay attention to your body's reaction and any hesitancy that arises. Chances are, the compliments you struggle to accept are the ones that you don't believe about yourself. This practice will give you a good sense of where you should focus your self-love journey in the beginning. This can also serve as an ongoing assessment to develop new goals.

PROMPT | In what ways do those around you demonstrate or communicate their love to you? In what ways would you like those around you to demonstrate or communicate their love to you?

### PRACTICE | **DROP AND GIVE ME SIXTY: A BREATHING MOMENT**

Black women have been holding their breath for centuries. This has severe impacts on both our mental and physical health. Consider this your reminder to breathe.

Unclench your jaw and loosen your shoulders. Inhale your visualization of self-love (this could be a bright light, an affirmation, etc.). Exhale your visualization of negative self-images (this could be darkness, negative self-talk, etc.). Do this for sixty seconds. Repeat as necessary.

As you grow into a new version of yourself, it's important to make room by clearing some of the things you've been holding on to. However, it's not always easy to let go of behaviors and fears, as they once served a purpose.

Use the following exercise to name a few behaviors, thoughts, and actions you wish to let go of as well as the purposes they previously served in your life.

**Example 1:** *I am letting go of self-sabotage, and I give gratitude for it keeping me in my comfort zone.*

**Example 2:** *I am letting go of stress eating, and I give gratitude for it making me feel better when I was overwhelmed.*

I am letting go of *[behavior/action/thought]* _____ ,

and I give gratitude for *[its purpose]* _____

I am letting go of _____ ,

and I give gratitude for _____

I am letting go of _____ ,

and I give gratitude for _____

I am letting go of _____ ,

and I give gratitude for _____

I am letting go of _____ ,

and I give gratitude for _____

I FULLY EMBRACE
AND LOVE
EVERY VERSION
OF MYSELF.

## KEY TAKEAWAYS

This section's goal was to create a good understanding of where you are starting in this journey and where you may need to focus some attention moving forward. We took a look at the ways we shield ourselves in this world and what we have done to survive until this point. It's up to you to lead your journey and decide what you wish to shift and what you wish to keep. Ultimately, the more you let go of, the more space you create to invite different things in. Things to take along your journey:

- You are enough, exactly as you are.

- You can fully embrace and love every version of yourself.

- You already possess talents, gifts, and positive traits that will be building blocks to unlock newer versions of yourself.

- At any moment you can assess where you are and where you want to go—your self-love goals should come from inside you and not anyone else.

# CHAPTER 5

# DISCOVER
# SELF-COMPASSION

Before we can step fully into loving ourselves, it's important to become aware of the way we view our behaviors and actions. We are at times our own biggest critics. We have the hardest time extending the same level of grace to ourselves as we do for others. When we make a mistake, we can be very hard on ourselves. These voices sometimes sound like "I should've known better" or "I am so stupid." This is where discovering self-compassion can be helpful. This means making yourself your biggest cheerleader. This is the opportunity to practice kindness, forgiveness, and respect for yourself. Grace and forgiveness are at the center of this part of your journey.

Nia is a twenty-six-year-old Black mama of two kids. Nia's children have different fathers, neither of whom Nia is in an active relationship with. Early in our sessions together, Nia carried so much shame and guilt about the choices she had made when she was younger. She consistently beat herself up about becoming a mother at a young age. She felt that because of her "poor decision-making" with her partners, she had ruined her children's lives. She thinks about how the partners she chose were a reflection of the lack of self-worth she felt. Since the fathers of her children weren't as present, she consistently felt like she wasn't doing enough to provide both physically and emotionally—even though she was the "full-time" parent. On top of all the shame and guilt she placed on herself, co-parenting was very stressful and further reinforced her "bad decision-making."

Using the exercises in this section, I had Nia explore self-compassion, grace, and forgiveness. In just a few short sessions, Nia began to discuss letting go of shame and guilt. She even discussed how doing this work has made her a more patient and attentive parent. And although co-parenting is still a challenge, Nia has learned to place the energy she used to use to shame herself back into caring for herself and her family.

# I AM WORTHY OF FORGIVENESS, COMPASSION, AND EMPATHY.

**WHAT'S THE EVIDENCE?**

Self-sabotage and negative self-talk are often the barriers impeding our ability to reach our higher selves—or the best person we can be. In what ways do you "self-sabotage," and what are the main thoughts associated with this? Identifying these habits is the first step in changing your behavior.

**Example:** *As I get closer to people in relationships, I begin to look for the "negative" and begin more conflict. The core belief I hold related to relationships is that "when people get too close, they hurt me, so I need to prove that I am strong."*

The following is a list of common negative beliefs and self-sabotage behaviors. Check the ones that feel relevant to you:

☐ Looking for the bad in all situations

☐ Believing things are too good to be true

☐ Spending outside my means

☐ Starting conflict in relationships when I get close to someone

☐ Isolating or pulling back

☐ Not putting intentional effort into my appearance

☐ Holding my tongue when I feel harmed

☐ "I am not good enough"

☐ "I am a bad person"

☐ "I don't deserve nice things"

☐ "All people will hurt me in some way"

☐ "All partners cheat"

☐ "I am supposed to be alone"

☐ "I don't deserve to be happy"

☐ "I ruin everything I come into contact with"

Write in any other core beliefs or things you may do to self-sabotage:

_____

_____

_____

_____

_____

_____

_____

_____

_____

_____

_____

_____

_____

_____

_____

_____

_____

_____

_____

_____

_____

_____

_____

PROMPT | What things are blocking you from achieving unconditional self-love? Consider the assessment you completed in the last section (page 62)—have you identified anything you may want to change? Blocks can be mental (limiting beliefs or thoughts), physical (wanting to change your appearance), or spiritual (not being grounded in spirituality or knowing who you are).

## PRACTICE | **STAYING GROUNDED: BUTTERFLY HUG**

While doing the work on your self-love journey, it is possible that you may become triggered or have big emotions emerge. It's important to continuously communicate to your body and yourself that you are okay and safe. The butterfly hug is adopted from trauma-informed practices that help people communicate to their bodies and brains that everything is okay.

Sitting in a comfortable position, with your palms facing your body, cross your arms and hold on to your opposite shoulders (left hand grabs right shoulder, right hand grabs the left). If you move your hands slightly below your shoulders, it can feel like you're giving yourself a hug. Now, just as a butterfly would flap its wings to fly, slowly tap one side of your body and then the other. Feel free to couple this with deep breathing and statements such as "I am okay" or "I am safe." You may do this for as long as you need to get grounded.

PROMPT | Think about the concept of "rupture and repair"—the notion that we will mess up and cause harm to others and ourselves, and while we need to take accountability for that, many things can be repaired. Was this modeled to you growing up? Often grace and forgiveness are hard to obtain if we've never really experienced them ourselves. Embracing this concept of "rupture and repair" allows us to be held accountable but also hold more grace with ourselves. Are there instances in your life when people have been able to successfully repair things with you?

_____

_____

_____

_____

_____

_____

_____

_____

_____

_____

_____

_____

_____

_____

_____

_____

## PRACTICE | **NOTES OF ENCOURAGEMENT: THE WRITING IS ON THE WALL**

As with learning any new skill or behavior, we can always use some motivation to keep going and affirmation that we are headed in the right direction. This practice will put you into the position of being your own biggest cheerleader, even when the journey gets tough.

Grab something to write with and on (I recommend a marker and sticky notes). Write down words of encouragement such as "You are exactly where you need to be" or "Trust the process"…whatever you think you need to hear when things get tough—these can even include the affirmations placed throughout this workbook. Strategically post these sticky notes in places you often spend time—your car, your office, the bathroom, and so on. The key is having consistent reminders that you are in your own corner.

Triggers are essentially strong emotional and often bodily reactions to a situation or stimulus in your environment. Understanding what triggers us is essential to controlling our response. Triggers can be broken up using our five senses.

Using the space provided, outline both positive and negative triggers for yourself and the emotions you associate with each. Try to include at least one each for sight, smell, touch, taste, and sound.

| SENSE | TRIGGER | EMOTIONAL REACTION |
|-------|---------|--------------------|
| Smell | smell of fresh-baked cookies reminds me of my grandmother's home | It makes me feel safe. |
|       |         |                    |
|       |         |                    |

| SENSE | TRIGGER | EMOTIONAL REACTION |
|-------|---------|--------------------|
|       |         |                    |
|       |         |                    |
|       |         |                    |
|       |         |                    |

PROMPT | Take a moment and think about your earliest memory of guilt and/or shame. Describe it here. Now think of the ways these feelings have influenced the way you show up in the world. Do they influence how you present, how you talk, who you hang around with? Exploring how guilt and shame have been taught to us can help us release the ways they may still control us.

## PRACTICE | **"AND THAT'S OKAY": GRACE IN ACTION**

Often how we talk about ourselves or our behaviors influences how we view them. It is easy to participate in negative self-talk and begin to put ourselves down. This practice will begin to help you shift how you talk about and eventually view your behaviors and actions.

This may seem silly at first, but when things don't go as planned or you come up short, think of ways to intentionally be compassionate. For example, instead of saying, "I have been lazy all day," try saying, "My body needed rest today, so I chose to honor that—and that's okay." Or maybe instead of "I am a cry baby," try "My body needs an emotional release, and that's okay." This is not meant to be avoidant or an attempt to evade accountability, but we all need a little love—and that's okay.

We often allow our emotional response to control our actions. I like to refer to these actions as our "emotional buttons." When you experience an emotion, you might react automatically. Learning to identify your buttons and process your immediate reactions can help you understand where those feelings are coming from and make them easier to control in the moment.

Write a list of your emotional buttons here, then follow the prompts to further explore your emotional buttons. This activity can be done with each emotional button. I encourage you to continue even after the prompts.

"My emotional buttons are pushed when . . ."

*. . . people talk down to me*

*. . . people are late*

*. . . my partner doesn't call me throughout the day*

_____

_____

_____

_____

_____

Now let's take one emotional button and look closer . . .

**Emotional Button:** *When people talk down to me*

**Thoughts:** *People think they are better than me and think I am stupid and less than.*

**Feelings:** *Inadequate, helpless, stupid, angry, unimportant, like a child, powerless*

**Memories:** *I remember when I was younger, my older sister always talked down to me and my mother didn't do anything to help.*

**Emotional Button:**

_____

**Thoughts:**

_____

_____

**Feelings:**

_____

_____

**Memories:**

_____

_____

Now let's see when these emotional buttons arise:

The people who are most likely to push this emotional button: _supervisors; my older siblings; my partner_

_____

I am more likely to react negatively when: _I am tired; I am being talked down to in front of other people_

_____

Another reaction could be: _Discuss my reaction using "I" statements; request that others reframe the way they are speaking; depersonalize the experience_

_____

_____

PROMPT | Think of a younger version of you. What are the things that little girl needed to be told or shown that would allow her to be more compassionate today?

_____

_____

_____

_____

_____

_____

_____

_____

_____

_____

_____

_____

_____

_____

_____

_____

_____

_____

_____

_____

_____

_____

Self-forgiveness is often difficult for Black women, but this is one of the keys to unlocking self-love. We are not perfect. We have made mistakes and likely harmed others in our journey. Acknowledging this is important, but we have to release the shame and guilt. We cannot call in grace from others without first extending it to ourselves. You are worthy of forgiveness.

Take a moment to outline places you will practice self-forgiveness.

*Example: "I forgive myself for staying in an unhealthy relationship because I thought it was love and didn't think I deserved more at the time."*

I forgive myself for _____

because _____

_____

_____

I forgive myself for _____

because _____

_____

_____

I forgive myself for _____

because _____

_____

_____

I forgive myself for _____

because _____

_____

_____

# I CAN RELEASE CHALLENGING EMOTIONS THAT HOLD ME DOWN SO THAT I CAN FLY.

# KEY TAKEAWAYS

Remember that self-love and self-compassion go hand in hand. The goal is to create harmony between forgiveness, grace, accountability, and responsibility. Remember that our feelings influence our thoughts and our thoughts guide our actions. You have power in each of those pieces. Approach your behaviors with nonjudgmental curiosity. Things to take away:

- You can release challenging emotions that hold you down so that you can fly.

- You are worthy of forgiveness, compassion, and empathy.

- Feelings give you information, but they may be distracting you from the facts.

- Acknowledging your mistakes creates space for accountability and forgiveness.

- Understanding your emotional buttons gives you the power to control your behaviors.

# CHAPTER 6

# LET GO OF SELF-DOUBT

Our thoughts are very powerful. Often the biggest obstacle we face is getting out of our own way. Negative self-talk and limiting beliefs drive what we do—or what we don't do—for ourselves. In this section, we will center around letting go of negative thoughts or self-limiting beliefs that we may hold about ourselves as Black women. When we are able to release and let go of self-doubt, we can stand in confidence. Increased confidence allows us to be grounded and rooted.

Ryan has been working with me for the past several months. She often describes her healing journey as a "roller coaster." In her eyes, she keeps going back to where we started. She learns boundaries but during very stressful times, she finds it hard to honor them. She learns effective communication skills but just can't seem to use them when she's triggered. Upon some further reflection and processing, Ryan has discovered how this process pokes at a core belief she holds about herself: "I will never be enough." Because she holds this belief, her actions start to align with it. When she finds stability, she is likely to self-sabotage because she figures she'll never be good enough. Her "roller coaster" experience was heavily influenced by her core beliefs. Ryan wasn't just born into the world believing that she wasn't "good enough"—it was a learned behavior. We discovered how her childhood experiences formed and reinforced this belief. Now we are on a quest to challenge old beliefs and invite new ones into Ryan's life. New beliefs lead to new thoughts, which ultimately lead to new actions.

# I TRUST
# MY INTUITION.

### PRACTICE | **STAYING GROUNDED IN REALITY: THE THREE Fs**

When you have lived a life full of second-guessing yourself, it's hard to be rooted in any reality. Discernment is a skill that can take a while to develop. This practice will hopefully allow you to begin seeing situations without the filter of self-doubt.

When you are faced with a potentially triggering situation, take a moment to slow down and assess what I like to call the three Fs: What are my FEARS? What are my FEELINGS? And what are the FACTS? From this standpoint, you can begin to make decisions with a clearer understanding. For example, I was offered a promotion, out of the blue, several months ago—this brought up so much for me and immediately triggered some self-sabotage behaviors (taking a long time to respond, feeling as if I needed to overexplain, etc.). Upon applying the three Fs, I uncovered my FEAR was that I would not be good enough and fail. My FEELINGS were inadequacy and anxiety. The FACTS were that I had earned that promotion and exhibited my willingness to serve, learn, and grow in and outside the workforce. It was from here that I was able to make an informed decision instead of allowing my self-doubt and self-sabotage to take over.

PROMPT | Often fear is at the center of scarcity-based decision-making. An example of scarcity-based decision-making is feeling like you have to continue working a job or staying in a toxic relationship because that's all you deserve or you fear that you are not worthy/qualified for anything more. Tap into your self-doubt and write down what your fears or blocks are to achieving confidence in yourself and your decision-making.

## EXERCISE | **FACTS OVER FEAR**

Gaslighting—making someone question their own reality—is a tool often used to manipulate someone into doubting themselves and their perceptions. Often, we become skilled at gaslighting ourselves—creating an environment of uncertainty. One of the best ways to combat gaslighting is to focus on the "facts." What are some things you *know* to be true about yourself? Are you kind? Are you patient? Often the evidence we have about ourselves helps keep us grounded.

Write a series of statements about things you fear. Based on each fear statement, provide a statement of fact that may go against the fear.

**Example:** Fear: *I am unlovable*
         Fact: *I am loved by my friends and partner*

**Fear**

_____

_____

_____

_____

_____

**Fact**

_____

_____

_____

_____

_____

PROMPT | Self-sabotage is the manifestation of self-doubt. For some, self-sabotaging behaviors bring a level of comfort because it can be reassuring to stay where you are. Change can be intimidating, even if it's ultimately for the best. Identify some behaviors you are likely to act on when you feel insecure. What are the effects of acting on those behaviors?

## PRACTICE | **WISDOM FROM WITHIN: A MEDITATIVE PRACTICE**

There are many versions of ourselves that exist in our minds, but often the one that pops out the most is born from our insecurities and fears. This practice will help you tap into the highest version of yourself where you can glean wisdom from within.

Find a comfortable and quiet space. Settle in and relax your body. Take a few deep breaths, in and out. Begin imagining a more confident, grounded version of yourself.

What does she look like?

Where is she (physically)?

What feelings arise when you look at her?

Imagine that you are meeting this version of yourself for the first time. Greet her with excitement; this could go something like "Hey, girl, hey!" or "It's the confidence and self-love for me!" Feel free to be as silly and authentic as you are led to be. Now that the highest version of you is here, the two of you are sitting across from each other, drinks in hand, keke'ing it up. But then it's time to get serious and ask her the questions you really want to know.

Now I invite you to ask her the following:

How did you get here?

What do I have to do in this moment to move past my self-doubt?

Feel free to ask your highest version more questions if they come up naturally, and when you are finished, thank her for her insight and wisdom. Take a moment to journal and reflect on your experience.

**PROMPT** | Write about a time where you let self-doubt take over. What was the outcome? Was it less than favorable? What would you do differently if you could? How can you remind yourself to check your self-doubt when in a triggering situation?

## EXERCISE | NOT RECOGNIZING THE WOMAN IN THE MIRROR

Imposter syndrome can be defined as having consistent self-doubt about your accomplishments, believing that you didn't earn a position or opportunity you have, and/or feeling like you may be exposed as a fraud. Black women experience imposter syndrome in many facets of their lives—at work, at home, and even among other Black women. Consistent self-doubt impedes our ability to reach new levels of self-love.

Using the following assessment, you can begin to uncover where you are with imposter syndrome.

1. I have a hard time accepting praise for my accomplishments.

☐ not at all ☐ rarely ☐ sometimes ☐ often ☐ very true

2. I am able to recall times that I made mistakes more than the times I felt proud of myself.

☐ not at all ☐ rarely ☐ sometimes ☐ often ☐ very true

3. I believe that the opportunities I have been afforded are a result of luck.

☐ not at all ☐ rarely ☐ sometimes ☐ often ☐ very true

4. I feel undeserving of the opportunities in my life.

☐ not at all ☐ rarely ☐ sometimes ☐ often ☐ very true

**5.** Those around me often have more confidence in my skills and ability than I do.

☐ not at all      ☐ rarely      ☐ sometimes      ☐ often      ☐ very true

**6.** I don't fully apply myself or seek out other opportunities.

☐ not at all      ☐ rarely      ☐ sometimes      ☐ often      ☐ very true

**7.** Those around me think that I am more competent than I am.

☐ not at all      ☐ rarely      ☐ sometimes      ☐ often      ☐ very true

**8.** I am afraid people will find out who I really am.

☐ not at all      ☐ rarely      ☐ sometimes      ☐ often      ☐ very true

**9.** I feel as if my success is due to luck.

☐ not at all      ☐ rarely      ☐ sometimes      ☐ often      ☐ very true

**10.** I often believe everyone around me is more competent than I am.

☐ not at all      ☐ rarely      ☐ sometimes      ☐ often      ☐ very true

Insecurity, in this context, can be defined as being uncertain or anxious about oneself—leading to a lack of confidence. In the moments we feel insecure, we allow feelings of uncertainty to lead our thoughts and actions. We often see these thoughts and actions present in our relationships—whether it's at work, with our children and partners, or even around our friends.

Next, name some insecurities you may have and piece out the ways they influence your behaviors and thoughts.

**Insecurity:** *Not finishing school*

**Feeling:** *Inadequate*

**Thoughts:** *"I am not smart enough"*

**Actions:** *I don't help my kids with homework; I don't apply for jobs I really want; I get defensive when asked about something I don't know*

**Impact:** *I come off as impatient with my kids; I don't challenge myself to enter spaces that may challenge me*

Insecurity: _____

_____

Feeling : _____

_____

Thoughts: _____

_____

Actions: _____

_____

Impact: _____

_____

Insecurity: _____

_____

Feeling : _____

_____

Thoughts: _____

_____

Actions: _____

_____

Impact: _____

_____


Insecurity: _____

_____

Feeling : _____

_____

Thoughts: _____

_____

Actions: _____

_____

Impact: _____

_____

PROMPT | Think about who you could be and what you are going to accomplish when you release self-doubt and insecurities. Write about what that would look like. How would you know you are moving in confidence?

_____

_____

_____

_____

_____

_____

_____

_____

_____

_____

_____

_____

_____

_____

_____

_____

_____

_____

_____

_____

_____

_____

_____

_____

Now that we have identified the areas where we are blocked, it's important to begin outlining a plan for where we want to be. Think of honoring your boundaries as a step beyond just setting them. To explain further, many of us have no problem setting boundaries—we get ourselves into sticky situations when we do not enforce or align with such boundaries. Honoring our boundaries is the bridge between knowing what we want and creating the steps to get there. Setting boundaries is simply communicating: "This is what I want or where I want to be." Honoring your boundaries is where you may align your actions, behaviors, and thoughts.

Next, outline where you would like to be and what alignment may look like.

| WHERE I WANT TO BE ... | HOW I WILL GET THERE ... |
|---|---|
| *"I want to feel more confident in my body."* | *"I will wear clothes that make me feel confident."* |
| | |
| | |
| | |
| | |
| | |

# I KNOW MYSELF, AND I AM CONFIDENT THAT I CAN MAKE DECISIONS IN MY OWN BEST INTEREST.

## KEY TAKEAWAYS

**W**ow! We did a lot of work in these sections! Kudos to you. Facing those negative thoughts and self-limiting beliefs is not an easy job. Although we will always combat a level of self-sabotage and limiting beliefs, we will have a better chance to recognize them and make the necessary shifts to align with where we want to be. Things to take with you:

- You know yourself and are confident that you can make decisions in your own best interest.

- You trust your intuition.

- Honoring your boundaries is the bridge between knowing what you want and creating the steps to get there.

- Use the three Fs—Fears, Feelings, and Facts—to assess and gain information.

# CHAPTER 7

# FOSTER YOUR SELF-WORTH

Now that we have identified and begun to release feelings of self-doubt, it's time to build self-love. This section will focus on your strengths, gifts, and talents. We will also begin to learn how to love our bodies and minds, despite what we've been taught about being Black women. Consider this for reclaiming your time and narrative: "Use what ya got to get what ya want!" The journey to self-love is not necessarily always about completely changing who you are and what you think. Sometimes it's putting the spotlight on what you already have and reframing your existing thoughts. If you got it, flaunt it, sis! Ready to keep going? Let's get started!

Cookie, a forty-eight-year-old woman, has been traveling along her self-love journey for some time now. When Cookie was young, she faced many obstacles with the other Black women in her life. Her grandmother made comments that her hair was "unkept" and "nappy." Her mother always criticized Cookie's developed physical features in an attempt to shame her for attracting male attention. Cookie got into many fights in school with other girls in her grade because they thought she was too "bougie." Cookie lived for many years with the pressure to look perfect before leaving the house, covering up just enough. Cookie kept to herself because she didn't know how to relate to other women, which came off as if she thought she was better than those around her. Cookie lived many years simply reacting to what the world had taught her about being a Black woman. Through the course of her self-exploration and self-love journey, Cookie has been able to identify and be intentional about how she shows up in this world. Furthermore, Cookie has been empowered with enough tools to help shape who she really wants to be. Cookie has come to embrace her unique hair texture and the ways her body naturally sits. And thanks to my girl Issa Rae, Cookie has settled into her personality as the "awkward Black girl"—but with pride instead of shame. While loving her whole self is still a process, Cookie has become the author of her own story. It's never too late.

# I WOKE UP LIKE THIS. BOW DOWN, BAD THOUGHTS.

PROMPT | Freewrite: I am beautiful because . . .

_____

_____

_____

_____

_____

_____

_____

_____

_____

_____

_____

_____

_____

_____

_____

_____

_____

_____

_____

_____

## PRACTICE | **GRATEFULNESS: MINDFUL MOMENT**

Practicing gratitude and mindfulness is helpful because it increases our ability to remain grounded, focused, and in control of our day-to-day. Mindfulness practices for my clients have helped reduce stress, anxiety, and emotional reactivity. Practicing gratitude helps you create pathways to internal joy and stillness—even in the midst of an external storm.

Use the following prompt to begin practicing gratitude and mindfulness: What is one thing you are grateful for right now? Picture this in your mind and allow those warm and fuzzy feelings to fill you up!

PROMPT | Write a love letter to yourself. Be sure to discuss the things you love about you, your body, and your personality.

_____

_____

_____

_____

_____

_____

_____

_____

_____

_____

_____

_____

_____

_____

_____

_____

_____

_____

_____

_____

_____

_____

_____

_____

_____

**BADASS BLACK WOMEN**

Have you ever done the activity in middle school where you spell your name and find words to describe yourself, starting with your first initial? It may have seemed silly then, but there's a lot of power in the language we use to describe ourselves, particularly as Black women. Well, there's no better time to take a blast to the past!

Using the letters provided, fill in words about what Black women are and how it feels to be a Black woman. Sidenote: You may have to head to Google or a thesaurus for this one. Throw this activity in the group chat and see how well your friends/family do! Then write out your name and do the same for words that personally describe you. Revisit this list when you need to remind yourself to practice self-compassion and self-love.

**B**  *"badass" ;)*

**L**  *lovely*

**A**  *authentic*

**C**

**K**

**W**

**O**

**M**

**E**

**N**

PROMPT | Freewrite: I am strong because . . .

"Comparison is the thief of joy" is a quote from Theodore Roosevelt, and while he is far from a Black woman, our friend Teddy was onto something. It can be detrimental to our self-esteem to compare what we have or don't have to others. It sends a message that we will never be or have enough—when in fact, that's a limiting belief. When we find ourselves focusing on what we don't have, we often miss the opportunities to celebrate what we do have. Despite the many obstacles we face, being a Black woman is lit! Being who you are, as you are, is your truest flex!

Take a moment to "brag" on yourself. What are the things about yourself that you are proud of and make you uniquely you? Follow these prompts:

**1.** Things I love about my body . . . _____

_____

_____

**2.** I am a good friend because . . . _____

_____

_____

**3.** My special talents include . . . _____

_____

_____

**4.** Things that bring me joy are . . . _____

_____

_____

**5.** I inspire myself because . . . _____

_____

_____

## PRACTICE | **COMBATING ANXIETY: SHAKE IT OFF**

There are levels of anxiety that are normal and weave their way into our lives. Anxiety is not inherently bad; it's our body's way of telling us something is wrong. It helps us stay alert and keep ourselves safe. The problem is when the anxiety overstays its welcome. Because anxiety can be a physical response, it's important to take a bodily approach to addressing the symptoms, as well as working on its underlying causes.

1. Recognize where anxiety lives in your body (examples: chest, tummy, shoulders).

2. What does it feel like? (examples: pins and needles, butterflies)

3. Shake it out: It may seem silly at first, but moving your body (like the inflatables in front of a car dealership) can help you release built-up anxiety.

4. Do this as many times or for as long as you need.

PROMPT | Write a list of people who you admire and look up to. What about them do you admire? In what ways do they practice self-love?

_____

_____

_____

_____

_____

_____

_____

_____

_____

_____

_____

_____

_____

_____

_____

_____

_____

_____

_____

_____

_____

## EXERCISE | TALKING BACK (THOUGHT BUBBLES VS. SPEECH BUBBLES)

You don't have to be a part of the Geto Boys to know when your mind may be playing tricks on you. Often our thoughts can lead to internalized feelings. Talking back is empowering.

Using the following thought and speech bubbles, think of the ways you can "talk back" to your negative thoughts with grace and empathy.

**Example:** Thought bubble: *"You are not physically attractive."*
Speech bubble: *"I am working on being comfortable in my body, but I still love where it is now."*

## PRACTICE | **INTENTIONAL EATING: SLOWING DOWN**

As Black women, we sometimes find ourselves on autopilot, living our days out from one task to another. Sometimes it's not easy to build in mindful moments or self-care, so this activity is to be used while doing something we have to do daily—eating.

Pick a mealtime and use this space to become more intentional. Focus on what you're eating. Chew slowly. Pick out all the different textures and tastes. Take a breath in between each bite. This may extend your normal mealtime by about five minutes but creates an opportunity to bring intentionality into your day without adding another task.

# EXERCISE | CELEBRATE YO' SELF PLAYLIST

We have discussed the importance of incorporating our five senses into our active healing. There is power in the things we consume. The food we eat can either nourish our body or bring it harm. The people we surround ourselves with can give us energy or drain us. The same goes for the media we take in. These things can uplift and speak light into us or diminish us and bring on darkness.

Let's work on a list of songs that celebrate your inner badass. Start your mornings off every day with this playlist and/or play it when self-doubt starts to kick up.

| SONG | WHAT'S THE MESSAGE FROM THIS SONG? |
|---|---|
| "Video" by India Arie | It's okay to be different and celebrate who you are. |
|  |  |
|  |  |
|  |  |
|  |  |
|  |  |
|  |  |

# I AM EVERYTHING I NEED TO BE, RIGHT NOW, IN THIS MOMENT.

# KEY TAKEAWAYS

It's the confidence and self-love for me! Taking time during this journey to celebrate ourselves and the work we have put in allows us to keep building on our foundation. As your journey continues, it's your strength and talents that will keep you going! Things to take along your journey:

- You are everything you need to be, right now, in this moment.

- You woke up like that, bow down bad thoughts.

- There is power in the language we choose to describe ourselves.

- Comparison is the thief of joy.

# CHAPTER 8

# BUILD A COMMUNITY THAT EMPOWERS YOU

I f you're a nerd like me, you've probably heard the saying "All great superheroes need a sidekick," but then you realize, not many (if any) of the female superheroes get sidekicks. Many of us *are* the sidekicks—swooping in at the last minute to save the day, without all the glory. It's tempting to go into business for yourself, lock yourself in a cave, and take the world into your own hands. But even Batgirl needed support. Here's the reality: You cannot save everyone and yourself. The Avengers, the Justice League, and every other club of costumes was built on that premise. Building a community of support will help you take down more bad guys than going it alone. The section is all about creating a community that empowers you as a Black woman and helping you heal and nurture your relationships with others.

Let me tell you the story of my friend Kim. If you looked up "Superwoman," "S on the chest," or "Captain Save-It-All"—you would see a picture of my dear friend Kim, posing effortlessly, with just the right amount of wind blowing. Kim has always been the "strong friend" and also the strong family member, partner, coworker, mom, and neighbor. Now, Kim has never seen this as a weakness—it was just a matter of fact. When fires begin to burn, call Kim and she'll put them out. The problem is that too many fires began to spark at the same time. Kim was consistently running back and forth to put out fires because she "could handle it." At one point in time, Kim got so used to being a firefighter that she didn't know how to be anything else. In reality, Kim was throwing herself in the fire, thinking, "I can handle this." She began to suffer small "burns." Sacrificing time with her kids, not eating enough, and barely sleeping. Kim wasn't even able to take care of her basic needs consistently. Eventually all the stress and putting out fires led her to a heart attack. It was at that time Kim learned the value of asking for help, building a solid support system, and letting go of her cape.

# I DESERVE TO BE HEARD, SEEN, AND SUPPORTED.

PROMPT | #RelationshipGoals. Relationship goals are the dynamics that inspire us and that we wish to obtain. Write a list of "relationship goals" that you have for the following: relationship with yourself, relationship with a partner, relationships with family, and relationship with friends. These can be specific dynamics or entire relationships. If you list a specific relationship, like "Pam and Gina," think about what characteristics of this relationship intrigue you.

## EXERCISE | CIRCLE OF INFLUENCE

Here is a series of circles, with you in the middle. Use this diagram to note who makes up your support system. Those in the sphere closest to the middle should represent the ones you are closest with or spend the most time with. Those in the sphere farther away should represent individuals who you are not close with or are distanced from. After you place your support system in their positions, do an assessment. Is there anyone who you want to move closer? Is there anyone who is too close? Would some people assume that they are closer/farther away? Are you satisfied with your circle of influence?

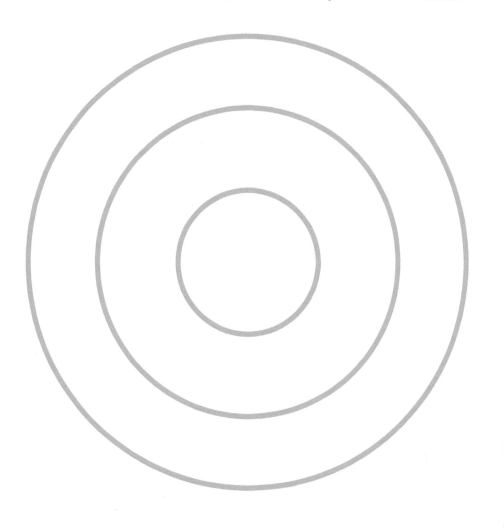

## PRACTICE | **LOVE NOTES: POSITIVE REINFORCEMENTS**

It's always the right time to express to someone how much we appreciate them. Depending on your love language, you could do this in different ways.

Take some time to write love notes to your support system. Be sure to note specific actions or situations that you are grateful for. Instead of "I am grateful for you," try "When you bring me food while I am working, it lets me know that you care about me."

PROMPT | Think of who takes up most of your time and energy on a daily basis. Does this relationship give you as much energy as it takes? Although many relationships are not always fifty-fifty, there should be harmony in the total amount of energy put in. In some dynamics, like parent-child relationships, one person will inherently consistently take more than they give. Where else can you receive energy if you are the caretaker in one or more of your relationships?

Many of the needs we have as humans are met through our relationships and interactions with others. However, no one person should be tasked to meet all your needs. Taking an assessment of what we get out of our relationships allows us to communicate if something is unsatisfactory.

Highlight three of your closest relationships and follow the prompts. Remember, it's your responsibility to communicate your needs.

**Example:**

Person I wish to highlight:  *Mom*

The energy exchange in the relationship is: ☐ unbalanced (I pour more)

☑ balanced (there is harmony)          ☐ unbalanced (they pour more)

This person is in my life because:  *she has always had my back*

This relationship has taught me:  *to be patient and forgiving*

The needs this relationship meets for me are:  *safety, stability, comfort*


**Relationship 1**

Person I wish to highlight: _____

The energy exchange in the relationship is: ☐ unbalanced (I pour more)

☐ balanced (there is harmony)          ☐ unbalanced (they pour more)

This person is in my life because: _____

This relationship has taught me: _____

The needs this relationship meets for me are: _____

## Relationship 2

Person I wish to highlight: _____

The energy exchange in the relationship is: ☐ unbalanced (I pour more)

☐ balanced (there is harmony)　　☐ unbalanced (they pour more)

This person is in my life because: _____

This relationship has taught me: _____

The needs this relationship meets for me are: _____

## Relationship 3

Person I wish to highlight: _____

The energy exchange in the relationship is: ☐ unbalanced (I pour more)

☐ balanced (there is harmony)　　☐ unbalanced (they pour more)

This person is in my life because: _____

This relationship has taught me: _____

The needs this relationship meets for me are: _____

## PRACTICE | **INTIMACY: MINDFUL MOMENT**

Take a moment to think about a time when you felt truly safe and vulnerable in a relationship. If you haven't, imagine what that might be like. Think of the ways you can incorporate safety and vulnerability into your relationships daily.

The amount of energy we "pour" into relationships will vary depending on life circumstances, but the key is harmony. If you find that you consistently pour into others more than they pour into you, this gives you information to make an informed decision about how much energy—if any—you should continue to give. The important thing is to have a good assessment that drives your decision-making. I have relationships in which the energy exchange is uneven—that does not necessarily mean that I will cut them completely out of my life, but I know which needs they are unable to meet for me. Use this activity as a relationship assessment to drive your decision-making.

Pictured here are a series of empty cups. Label two cups for each person in your support system. Consider how much each person "pours" into you. For the first cup, shade in the amount of energy that individual pours into you. Do they give you a full cup of energy or very little? On the next cup assigned to that person, consider how much energy your pour into them. How do those amounts compare? What changes might you want to make in each relationship with this information in mind?

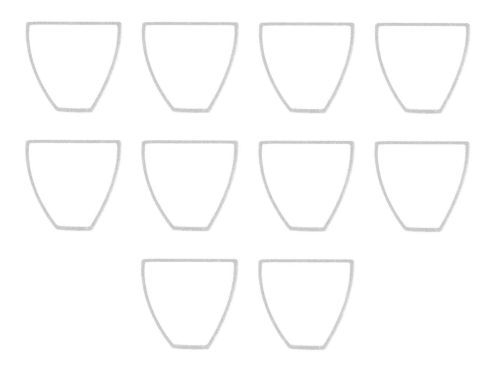

### PRACTICE | **BOUNDARY WORK IS HEALING WORK**

Boundaries help communicate and teach others about what you value and how to treat you. Having relationships and communities that honor and respect your boundaries is a pathway to safe and healthy connections.

Keep these tips in mind if you find yourself struggling to set or hold boundaries:

- Remember, boundaries are for *you* and not others.

- Instead of thinking of boundaries as saying *no* to someone else, think of them as saying *yes* to yourself.

- Continue to check in with your body. Often your body will give you information on things you may need to set a boundary around.

- Have *grace* with yourself. Your boundaries will shift and grow as you shift and grow.

PROMPT | Rupture and repair is a concept that all healthy relationships should embrace. It's the notion that accepts everyone isn't perfect and we will all make mistakes, but it's the effort put into the repair that can make or break a relationship. (Please note that this concept is not applicable for any form of physical, emotional, or psychological abuse.) Everyone's road to repair can look different, so outline the ways in which repair would be impactful for you. What would someone say or do that communicates a repair attempt? (You may consider how your love language influences this process.)

Sometimes the thing that prevents us from building and growing healthier relationships is the past pain and harm we have experienced. Many Black women have faced relationships that broke trust, lost respect, and maybe even threatened our physical, emotional, and psychological safety. It's hard to see ourselves in a healthy dynamic with friends, family, or a partner when the world has taught us not to trust. However, we deserve to experience intimate, joyful, and healthy relationships. By releasing pent-up hurt, anger, and pain, you are taking responsibility for your healing process.

Using the following prompts, pen a letter to someone who may have caused you harm in the past. You can use this framework anytime.

Dear _____,

You hurt me by _____

_____

This made me feel _____

_____

This made me think (about myself) _____

_____

But these are the facts: _____

_____

I have found support by _____

_____

I am not responsible for your hurting me. I am recovering from this. This does not control me. I deserve healthy relationships.

# IT'S NOT THEIR JOB TO LOVE ME. IT'S MINE.

# KEY TAKEAWAYS

It is in relationships that true healing begins to take place. You can tell yourself that you embody self-love, but self-love in practice shows up in how we interact with others. Setting boundaries is necessary to protect the work we have put in for ourselves. Letting go of past hurt and pain allows us to free up space and welcome something new. You are worthy of a community that shows up for you the same way you show up for yourself. Things to take along your journey:

- You deserve to be heard, seen, and supported.

- It's not their job to love you. It's yours.

- We deserve to experience intimate, joyful, and healthy relationships.

- No one person can meet your needs.

# CHAPTER 9

# COMMIT TO SELF-LOVE IN THE DAYS TO COME

What a journey! Here we are, transitioning into the final pieces of this workbook, and although we are wrapping up this piece of our journey, the marathon continues. In this section, we will reflect on the growth you've made, begin to ground you in dreams and goals, and enhance your courage to continue tackling any roadblocks that arise as you move along. I encourage you to put any new skills, language, and mindset shifts you have gained to use. Remember, if at first you don't succeed . . . dust yourself off and try again! Revisit this workbook as often as you need! You may find that your answers to the prompts change as you reach different points of your journey. Let's go for one more round!

Toni has been a longtime client. For several years, I have been a witness to her overcoming obstacles as they arise. Toni and I have tackled negative self-talk, trauma processing, setting boundaries, letting go of friends and family, and even processing how she chooses to show up as a Black woman in this world. Our sessions have moved from heavy crying and combating painful memories to celebrating her existence. Toni has begun to practice gratitude and mindfulness regularly. She has released her limiting beliefs and fear-based decision-making processes. She is learning to embrace vulnerability to fight through her anxiety and depression. Toni believes that she deserves the life on the other side of anxiety, self-sabotage, and toxic relationships. She has committed to showing up as her better self, even when it is difficult. Although Toni has more work to uncover, her foundation is strong. At one point in time, it felt impossible for Toni to be who she is today. Toni has created her own reality. Not only was it possible, it was destiny.

I AM A COMPLEX MASTERPIECE THAT KEEPS UNFOLDING EVERY DAY.

PROMPT | We have discussed a lot in these last several chapters. You may have applied new skills and concepts throughout our time together. It's important to look back and celebrate our progress, not matter how small we may feel it is. Reflect on one shift you have made since beginning this workbook.

_____

_____

_____

_____

_____

_____

_____

_____

_____

_____

_____

_____

_____

_____

_____

_____

_____

_____

_____

_____

_____

_____

## REFLECTING SELF-LOVE

This is another practice that you can add into your routine to be sure you are centering your self-love journey. We sometimes look to others to tell us what they like or admire about us, and although this can be extremely affirming, imagine how affirming it would be to hear these things regularly—from your own mouth. Here's a way to achieve that in five minutes or less: Look in the mirror every morning and say three things you love about yourself!

It's easy to get caught up in the business of life and begin to slack on the goals we set forth. You may find yourself a few months down this road, not implementing any self-care routines. Having a way to track helps create accountability and discipline.

Use the tracker provided or a similar one to keep yourself on task!

How am I feeling today or this week?

_____

_____

What is one thing I am grateful for today or this week?

_____

_____

What are some ways I showed self-love today or this week?

_____

_____

_____

What is my plan for self-care today or this week?

_____

_____

What is one boundary I'll set today or this week?

_____

_____

PROMPT | How do you plan to intentionally prioritize yourself and your healing journey moving forward?

_____

_____

_____

_____

_____

_____

_____

_____

_____

_____

_____

_____

_____

_____

_____

_____

_____

_____

_____

_____

## EXERCISE | SELF-LOVE LOVE LANGUAGE

"Love languages" is a concept that everyone receives and gives differently. This was coined by Gary Chapman in his book *The 5 Love Languages,* which offers a supplemental quiz for you to begin to understand your own love languages. I recommend that you take or revisit the quiz here: 5lovelan-guages.com. We often hear about the importance of love languages when referring to interpersonal relationships, but what about your relationship with yourself? Be sure you are speaking your *own* love languages when doing self-care activities.

Circle the self-care activities that you have or will be incorporating into your practice.

**Quality Time:**

- Spend time in the sun/outdoors

- Watch your favorite movie

- Color or paint

- Take care of plants/garden

- Go for a walk or hike

**Physical Touch:**

- Spend time on your hair or skin-care routine

- Stretch/yoga

- Cuddle with pillows or stuff animals

- Pet a dog

- Massage your scalp, hands, or feet

**Acts of Service:**

- Set monthly goals

- Declutter

- Volunteer

- Prep your lunch

- Schedule monthly "resets" to clean or catch up on work

**Words of Affirmation:**

- Use positive affirmations

- Listen to your favorite inspirational podcast

- Write yourself a love note

- Compliment yourself

- Keep a gratitude jar

**Receiving Gifts:**

- Schedule a monthly flower delivery

- Buy yourself lunch

- Take a course or class

- Invest in your hobbies

- Purchase one thing from your wish list monthly or quarterly

PROMPT | We all face challenges and barriers during our journey. Some believe that there is no triumph without tribulation. As I have stated many times before, focusing on the *process* just as much as the *product* will yield greater results and satisfaction. Take a moment to reflect on what challenges you anticipate during your process. For every challenge you name, try to list two or three "action items" or ways you can manage or tackle them as they arise.

## PRACTICE | **5-4-3-2-1**

If you haven't noticed, we like to hype ourselves up over here! This is a practice you can incorporate daily or weekly. It's a way to continuously put your strengths and assets at the center of your life. This can be a tool to prompt deeper self-discovery or to simply remind yourself to be your first priority.

Follow the prompts provided—you can journal them or use them as conversation starter with yourself or others.

**5** things I did well this week/day/month

**4** positive qualities I have

**3** achievements I have made

**2** things I have learned about myself

**1** thing I love about myself

EXERCISE | **SELF-CARE IN ACTION**

Self-care is a spectrum of things we do to pour love and appreciation into ourselves. It ranges from the basic things we do to survive (eating, sleeping) all the way to the things we perceive to be luxuries (massages, bubble baths, vacations). Often, Black women don't have a good balance in their self-care methods—if they do any self-care at all. This activity breaks down self-care as a holistic spectrum.

In each row, outline things you already do or would like to do for self-care. This exercise is adapted from the Olga Phoenix Project: Healing for Social Change. Referencing their prefilled self-care wheel can be helpful if you get stuck (see References, page 156).

**PHYSICAL**

**EMOTIONAL**

| PSYCHOLOGICAL | SPIRITUAL | PERSONAL | PROFESSIONAL |
|---|---|---|---|
| | | | |
| | | | |

Sometimes we beat ourselves up and get discouraged when we feel like we have not met our goals or made any progress. Instead of slipping back into negative-self talk, let's embrace the power of yet. Instead of saying "I don't love my body," try "I don't love my body, yet." This may seem like a small shift, but it opens the door to build and plan.

Use the following goal planning prompts to identify where you can place the power of "yet."

I am not good at _____ yet, but I will take these

steps: _____

_____

_____

_____

I don't know how to _____ yet, but I can

begin by _____

_____

_____

_____

I am not strong enough to _____ yet, but I will get

there by _____

_____

_____

_____

PROMPT | A newer version of yourself is evolving. As you shift and grow, your environment will begin to change as well. What are the differences between you and this version of yourself? Finish this prompt: "Allow me to reintroduce myself . . ."

EXERCISE | **GOAL SETTING**

Whew, it's been quite a journey. It may have taken you weeks or months to make it through this workbook. We have uncovered so much about where we are in our journey and where we wish to go. Here's the reality—many of these shifts and practices cannot be incorporated all at the same time, overnight. This will take time and practice. This exercise is meant to help you pare down your self-care goals to focus on at this moment.

You may have compiled a list of self-care goals throughout this workbook. Take a look back and pick out the top three you feel like you have the tools to begin or continue to work through.

My top three self-care goals are:

1. _____

2. _____

3. _____

Now that you have at least one goal to work toward, it's time to call on the community of support. Remember that an accountability partner is someone who values the same goals and will offer you nonjudgmental space in the way you need it. Take a moment to name an accountability partner—also be sure to let that person know that you have chosen them as your accountability partner for the specific goals you just outlined.

My accountability partner is: _____

I will revisit these goals by: _____

_____

_____

I will know when I reach these goals because: _____

_____

_____

THE LOVE I HAVE
FOR MYSELF IS
UNAPOLOGETIC,
UNCONDITIONAL,
AND UNWAVERING.
PERIOD.

## KEY TAKEAWAYS

**W**ow—if no one has told you this recently, please allow me: I am so proud of you! In this section, we discussed the value of goal setting, enriching the relationship with yourself, and the power of grace and patience in this journey. Here are your final takeaways:

- You are a complex masterpiece that keeps unfolding every day.

- The love you have for yourself is unapologetic, unconditional, and unwavering. Period.

- Leave the door open by embracing the power of "yet."

- Your self-care should be holistic.

- This journey may not be easy, but it's worth it.

# A FINAL WORD

WOOT! WOOT! *Insert praise dance* Look at you go! Congratulations! Welcome to the end of this workbook! I am glad you are here. You are meant to be here, right now, reading these words. I don't know the battles you fought to get here, but I sure am glad you made it out on the other side. Or if you're still going through it, know you will come out better for it at the end. You have done so much important and valuable work through these pages, and of course there's much more to go. Remember to trust the process. Refer back to the affirmations throughout each chapter. When you believe the words you say, you bring them to life. If you don't believe them at first, keep saying them until you do! Continuing this journey to self-love will yield great results. You will be able to walk in purpose, give love without strings attached, be kinder to yourself, and enjoy happier and healthier relationships. When you have a foundation of self-love, you begin to be more intentional in all areas of your life. You'll want to thank your body and feed it things that make it feel better. You'll strive for financial wellness and balance. You will look for relationships that add to your peace and joy. You will be grounded and firm in who you are and wish to be. There's not bigger flex than true self-love.

To our friends Jenesis, Melanie, Akela, Oya, Nia, Ryan, Cookie, Kim, and Toni—thank you for being yourselves, doing the work, and showing other Black women like us that self-love is achievable and necessary.

Sis, keep going. Things may get tough, and you may feel as if you're moving backward at times, but please push through and know that you are not alone. Sis, keep going. Self-love is not easy, but it's worth it—if you get discouraged, imagine what is on the other side of hurt, pain, anxiety, limiting beliefs, and toxic relationships. Sis, keep going. On the nights where the negative voices are just too loud and the darkness seems to be endless, look inside yourself to find stillness and light. Sis, keep going. And I will, too—know that you are the reason why this workbook was created in the first place. You are seen, you are not alone, you are the inspiration.

I'd love to hear about your journey and what pieces helped you! Please stay connected—you can find me on Instagram @halfhoodhalfholistic. See you soon, sis!

# RESOURCES

Hey, y'all! Throughout the text I dropped a few gems and referenced some awesome resources for additional growth. From microaggression to racial trauma to love languages, this workbook just gave a quick overview. Please find some of my favorite resources that I personally use in my work day-to-day—there are many books because I am a nerd and book collector. Allow these resources to introduce other areas of growth related to self-love.

1. TherapyforBlackgirls.com (resource directory and podcast)

2. *My Grandmother's Hands* by Resmaa Menakem (book)

3. Anything by bell hooks; *Sisters of the Yam* is a good starting point (book)

4. *Pleasure Activism* by Adrienne Maree Brown (book)

5. *The Racial Healing Handbook* by Anneliese A. Singh (book)

6. *Meditation Mixtape* by Shelah Marie (album)

7. *The Five Love Languages* by Gary D. Chapman (book) and 5lovelanguages.com (quiz)

8. Attachment Style Quiz: attachmentproject.com (resource and quiz)

9. Shine App: theshineapp.com (app)

10. Alkeme Health: alkemehealth.com (app)

11. Black Girls Smile: blackgirlssmile.org (organization and website)

12. Black Girls Can Heal: @blackgirlscanheal (organization and Instagram)

13. *Sacred Woman* by Queen Afua (book)

# REFERENCES

Bailey, Rahn Kennedy, Josephine Mokonogho, and Alok Kumar. 2019.
"Racial and Ethnic Differences in Depression: Current Perspectives."
*Neuropsychiatric Disease and Treatment* 15 (February 22, 2019): 603–9.
ncbi.nlm.nih.gov/pmc/articles/PMC6390869.

Burgess, Sam. "Learn Your Emotional Buttons." *Medium*. July 5, 2021.
medium.com/work-better-live-smarter/learn-your-emotional-buttons
-5323e76e0816.

Chapman, Gary D. *The 5 Love Languages: How to Express Heartfelt
Commitment to Your Mate*. Chicago: Northfield Pub, 1995.

International Society for Traumatic Stress Studies. "Public Resources."
Accessed February 18, 2022. istss.org/public-resources.

Jones, Holly J., Tamilyn Bakas, Sheila Nared, Jacqueline Humphries, Julie
Wijesooriya, and Melina Butsch Kovacic. 2022. "Co-Designing a Program to
Lower Cardiovascular Disease Risk in Midlife Black Women." *International
Journal of Environmental Research and Public Health* 19, no. 3 (January 26,
2022): 1356. ncbi.nlm.nih.gov/pmc/articles/PMC8835512.

King-White, Dakota, and Kristen Fuller. "Intergenerational Trauma: What It
Is & How to Heal." *Choosing Therapy*. Last modified April 6, 2022.
choosingtherapy.com/intergenerational-trauma.

Mental Health America. "Black and African American Communities and
Mental Health." mhanational.org/issues/black-and-african-american
-communities-and-mental-health.

Michals, Debra. "Mary Church Terrell." *National Women's History Museum*.
2017. womenshistory.org/education-resources/biographies/mary-church
-terrell.

Nelson, Tamara, Naysha N. Shahid, and Esteban V. Cardemil. "Do I Really Need to Go and See Somebody? Black Women's Perception of Help-Seeking for Depression." *Journal of Black Psychology* 46, no. 4 (June 5, 2020): 263–86. journals.sagepub.com/doi/full/10.1177/0095798420931644.

Phoenix, Olga. "Self-Care Wheel." OlgaPhoenix.com. 2013. olgaphoenix.com/self-care-wheel.

Zur, Ofer. "Understanding and Treating Intergenerational Transmission of Trauma." Zur Institute. Accessed February 18, 2022. zurinstitute.com /course/intergenerational-trauma.

# INDEX

# Acknowledgments

To have a brief Kanye West moment, I would like to express gratitude to myself first and foremost. I am so proud of you, baby girl, for all the work you have done for yourself that allows you to help others do their work.

There is a head nod to influential Black women throughout this book—the ones who have shaped and inspired my path. I am grateful.

And to my clients, it's only through you sharing your words and experiences that I am able to craft spaces just like these. I am honored, tribe.

Finally—Dexter, Bruce, Walida, LeeAnn, Jelilat, Ani, Tauri, Allana, Kayla, Jazmyn, Jennise, Malaysia, Dee Dee, Jerrett, Akela, Toni, Anthony, Hiram, Caleb, and Grayson—you all kept me grounded, focused, and determined.

# About the Author

**RACHEL JOHNSON**, LMSW, MFT, is a licensed mental health practitioner, doula, speaker, and activist who is passionate about enhancing the lives of the Black community through health and wellness. Rachel owns Half Hood Half Holistic—a holistic wellness brand centering accessible mind, body, and spirit healing for the Black community. Through advocacy, workshops, and trainings, Rachel is changing the face of maternal and mental health support for Black individuals across the United States. Much of Rachel's passion is in community-based nonprofit organizations. She has been on a mission to create culturally relevant, community-based programs that center mental and holistic wellness.

# NOTES

# NOTES